STRENGTH FOR THE
BROKEN PLACES

"*Strength for the Broken Places* invites us to confront our vulnerabilities, wounds, and scars with the hope and courage born of divine grace. Jim Harnish takes us on a journey into our own brokenness and gently leads us toward a new future of transformation and wholeness made possible by God's grace. This is a book to read and share with others!"
—**Kenneth L. Carder**, Williams Distinguished Professor of the Practice of Christian Ministry, Duke Divinity School, and United Methodist bishop

"James Harnish offers methods for identifying and dealing with our brokenness in a way that soothes the most difficult places while letting the reader in on the fact that these are common human experiences."
—**Trudie Kibbe Reed**, President, Bethune-Cookman University

"Jim Harnish insightfully tackles those issues that confront us all: sin and suffering that cause, perpetuate, and intensify brokenness in our lives and in our world. Yet this is a profoundly hopeful book, offering strength and encouragement when and where we need it most. A great book to use in small groups."
—**L. Gregory Jones**, Dean, Duke Divinity School

"Jim Harnish has written a book of incredible hope. This is a book that one will read with confession and gratitude for healing and then be compelled to share the message of living hope with others."
—**H. Eddie Fox,** World Director of Evangelism, World Methodist Council

"Jim Harnish has written a book that addresses the brokenness that we all seem to be increasingly experiencing. Every time I turn around I am hearing about something tragic in another's life, and I devoured this book during one of those moments in my own. I came away from reading this book with hope."
—**Nancy Rich**, Duke Divinity School

"Jim Harnish exposes all of us to the core of our being, uncovering every broken place we have worked hard to cover. Providing real examples of hurt, pain, and sin, he enables us to see the places of pain in our own lives—but he does not allow us to stay. Take out a journal and read along, bring to light the places of pain in your own life, and allow them to be healed."
—**Donna Claycomb Sokol,** Pastor, Mount Vernon Place United Methodist Church, Washington, DC

Strength for the Broken Places

James A. Harnish

Abingdon Press
Nashville

STRENGTH FOR THE BROKEN PLACES

Copyright © 2009 by Abingdon Press

This book is printed on acid-free paper.

Library of Congress Cataloging-in-Publication Data

Harnish, James A.
  Strength for the broken places / James A. Harnish.
    p. cm.
  ISBN 978-0-687-65763-6 (binding pbk., trade pbk., adhesive-perfect: alk. paper)
  1. Deadly sins. 2. Consolation. 3. Christian life—Methodist authors. I. Title.

  BV4626.H36 2009
  248.8'6—dc22

2009006737

All scripture quotations unless otherwise noted are taken from the New Revised Standard Version of the Bible, copyright 1989, Division of Christian Education of the National Council of the Churches of Christ in the United States of America. Used by permission. All rights reserved.

Scripture quotations marked (NIV) are taken from the Holy Bible, NEW INTERNATIONAL VERSION®. Copyright © 1973, 1978, 1984 by International Bible Society. All rights reserved throughout the world. Used by permission of International Bible Society.

Scripture quotations marked (NEB) are taken from *The New English Bible*. © The Delegates of the Oxford University Press and The Syndics of the Cambridge University Press 1961, 1970. Reprinted by permission.

Scripture quotations marked (RSV) are taken from the Revised Standard Version of the Bible, copyright 1952 [2nd edition, 1971] by the Division of Christian Education of the National Council of the Churches of Christ in the United States of America. Used by permission. All rights reserved.

Scripture quotations marked The Message are taken from *THE MESSAGE*. Copyright © by Eugene H. Peterson 1993, 1994, 1995, 1996, 2000, 2001, 2002. Used by permission of NavPress Publishing Group.

Scripture quotations marked (JBP) are taken from *The New Testament in Modern English*, rev. ed., trans. J. B. Phillips (Macmillan Publishing). © J. B. Phillips 1958, 1959, 1960, 1972.

Scripture quotations marked (ESV) are from The Holy Bible, English Standard Version®, copyright © 2001 by Crossway Bibles, a publishing ministry of Good News Publishers. Used by permission. All rights reserved.

Scripture quotations marked (NLT) are taken from the *Holy Bible*, New Living Translation, copyright © 1996. Used by permission of Tyndale House Publishers, Inc., Wheaton, Illinois 60189. All rights reserved.

09 10 11 12 13 14 15 16 17 18 — 10 9 8 7 6 5 4 3 2 1
MANUFACTURED IN THE UNITED STATES OF AMERICA

The world breaks everyone
and afterward many are strong
at the broken places.

       —Ernest Hemingway, *A Farewell to Arms*

Contents

Introduction

I'm broken. So are you. We're all broken people who live in a broken world. The critical question is how we find strength to put broken things back together again. Ernest Hemingway captured the reality of our brokenness and the hope of our healing in one of his most memorable sentences: "The world breaks everyone and afterward many are strong at the broken places" (*A Farewell to Arms*, Arrow, 2004, page 222).

This book is the invitation to touch the scars that mark the broken places in our lives just the way the Risen Christ invited a doubting disciple named Thomas to touch the nail scars in his hands. It is a challenge to explore some of the dark places in our human experience, to track down the sneaky culprit of temptation, to uncover the sinister power of sin, and to experience the way the grace of God, revealed at the cross, meets us in our broken places to bring new life through the power of the Resurrection.

With an opening like that, some readers might expect this book to be a dreary collection of sorrowful stories of broken hearts or shattered dreams. For others, it might conjure up images of judgmental preachers frothing at the mouth about the power of sin or of self-righteous prudes looking down their noses at fallen sinners.

Liza Hamilton was one of those people. John Steinbeck described her as "a tight hard little woman humorless as a chicken. She had a dour Presbyterian mind and a code of morals that pinned down and beat the brains out of nearly everything that was pleasant to do" (*East of Eden,* Penguin Books, 1981; page 10). I've known people like that, and they weren't all Presbyterians! My guess is that they are sincere in their desire to defeat the darkness and purge the world of sin, but I've never wanted to travel anywhere with them, least of all into the shadowy corners of my own soul. They aren't the kind of people with whom I would feel safe to reveal the broken places in my life.

Other readers may not be all that keen on seeing what lies beneath the carefully placed bandages that hide the scars of the past. We may be afraid of what we might find if we open the long-locked doors of broken hopes or disappointed dreams. Most of us have closets that contain skeletons we'd rather not disturb. We may not be ready to confront some newly raised Lazarus, dragging his grave clothes out of the tomb. (See John 11:43-44.)

My word of encouragement is that while this book begins in the darkness, it ends in the light. It's about the way the grace of God brings strength in our broken places. It's an invitation to experience the unexpected grace that meets us in the darkness with a light that can never be put out.

William Cowper (1731–1800) knew about broken places. For most of his life he suffered severe bouts of depression, in those days known as "melancholia." He spent eighteen years in the parish at Olney, England, with John Newton, the poet-priest who wrote "Amazing Grace." During those years, Cowper penned some of the most beautiful texts of British hymnody. In one of the most autobiographical, he described the light of God's grace breaking into the oppressive darkness in his life when he wrote

> Sometimes a light surprises
> The Christian while he sings;
> It is the Lord, who rises
> With healing in His wings:
>
> When comforts are declining,
> He grants the soul again
> A season of clear shining,
> To cheer it after rain.
> (*The Methodist Hymnal*, Methodist Publishing House, 1964, no. 231)

With confidence in the way the light of Christ is able to surprise us along the way, I invite you to explore some of the ways the world breaks all of us with the expectation that the surprising grace of God will give us new strength to confront the broken places in each of our lives.

To accomplish that goal, this book is biblical. This does not mean that it offers Bible verses as spiritual Band-Aids to cover over our wounds or that it prescribes biblical pills to explain away every pain. It means that I believe that when we enter deeply into the stories of scripture, we discover ways in which the Spirit of God meets us "with sighs too deep for words" (Romans 8:26), so that the written word becomes a living Word and God's presence becomes a "means of grace" in our experience.

It may come as a surprise to some readers to discover that the bulk of the Bible is not composed of theological doctrine, apologetic teaching, or practical principles for making life work a little better. Instead, most of the Bible is composed of stories: stories of the way God intersected with real human experience; stories of people like us; stories that invite our participation. And the story is often energized with song. Music flows through the stories like the songs in a Broadway musical. Miriam sings about God's deliverance through the Red Sea. Zechariah sings about the dawning of God's mercy in the birth of John. Mary sings about God's grace in the anticipation of the birth of Jesus. Angels sing to the shepherds the good news of Christ's birth. Paul and Silas sing their praises in prison. The hosts of heaven sing of the fulfillment of God's salvation in the Revelation.

The biblical message is carried by story and celebrated with song. So, my intent is to invite the reader to participate with me in listening to the story of scripture, so that through the written word, the Word made flesh will be made flesh in us. Because songs hold such a strong place in scripture and in my own spiritual journey, we'll include some of them along the way, too.

This book is also personal. Nothing connects with our lives as deeply as the story of the way particular people at a particular time found strength to face a particular broken place in their lives. All great works of literature, art, and drama are rooted in the story of the struggles and successes, joys and failures that are a part of the larger story of our common humanity.

One of the great stories of American history tracks the heroic pilgrimage of the Corps of Discovery to the Pacific Ocean under the leadership of Meriwether Lewis and William Clark. In his classic account of the expedition, Stephen E. Ambrose describes Lewis and Clark's "ability to get more out of the men than the men ever thought they could give." Every time the Corps overcame what appeared to be an impossible obstacle, "the men agreed that it had to be the worst, and that they could not possibly endure anything worse. Only to have it get worse." Sometimes *our* stories feel that way, too. "But," Ambrose writes, "well-led men working together can do far more than they ever thought they could. . . . [Lewis] knew they had more in them than they thought, and he knew how to bring out the best in them" (*Undaunted Courage*, Touchstone Books, 1996, pages 272-73).

God's self-revelation in scripture is rooted in the personal stories of particular people who experienced the presence of God in a particular time and a particular way. As we participate in the stories of the way God's grace brought out the best in them, we may discover that there is more within us than we thought, and we may find strength to overcome the challenges of our lives.

This book grows out of my spiritual journey through thirty-five years of pastoral experience in local congregations where I have participated in the stories of broken people who have found strength to face the broken places in their lives. It is a personal witness to the way the Spirit of God brought out the best in them in the worst situations. It also invites the reader into some of the broken places in my life in the hope that through the witness of God's grace at work in our experience, that same grace will become a reality for others.

I am grateful for the broken people who have helped me face my own brokenness. Like the writer of the 16th Psalm, the "lines have fallen for me in pleasant places" and I have been surrounded by "holy ones . . . in whom is all my delight" (Psalm 16:6, 3). I give thanks for the staff and congregation of Hyde Park United Methodist Church, Tampa, Florida, in whose fellowship these chapters first took shape; for Jim and Celia Ferman, in whose Crystal River hideaway the first draft of this book was written; for the nine guys in my clergy covenant group, with whom I have shared this journey for twenty-six years; and, as always, for my wife and family, who never hesitate to point out my broken places and give me strength to face them.

Like Uzziah, the sixteen-year-old king of Judah, it must be said of me, "he was marvelously helped until he became strong" (2 Chronicles 26:15).

—James A. Harnish

CHAPTER ONE
Scar Lover: The Signs of What We've Been Through

The wound must not be bandaged over as fast as possible; it is there to be a listening post, a chance to exit the small confines of a self-defined world and enter the spaciousness of a God-defined world.

—*Eugene H. Peterson,* Subversive Spirituality

I've never read the book. After reading the *New York Times* review, I quickly concluded that the perverse violence of Harry Crews's novel *Scar Lover* (Touchstone, 1993) was not exactly my idea of a good time. But I've never been able to forget the title, nor the way the reviewer described a scar as a sign of healing. The reviewer acknowledged that scars are often ugly. They sometimes remain tender to the touch. But scars are also evidence that the injury is in the past. They are the reminder of what we have been through. They remind us of where we've been. They mark us ever after for who we are.

I see a lot of scars in my business. Having logged my full share of post-surgery pastoral visits, I never cease to be amazed by the number of patients who insist on showing me their scars, sometimes in the most unexpected places! In fact, I've sometimes been tempted to show them mine! My scar is still there, tucked away where no one can see, the ugly reminder of abdominal surgery three decades ago. Long after the wound was healed, the scar remains.

Although I always try to be impressed when patients lift their hospital gowns to display their scars, I haven't seen a pretty one yet. I suspect the reason they want me to see the scars has something to do with the way a scar traces what they've been through. Even when tender to the touch, it can be a sign of healing. It reminds them of where they've been and who they are.

"Scar Lover." That odd name linked in my imagination with a peculiar detail in the post-Resurrection stories. Luke tells us that when the Risen Christ appeared to his disciples, "he showed them his hands and his feet" (Luke 24:40). John records that Christ "showed them his hands and his side" (John 20:20). Both Gospels agree that the Risen Christ showed the disciples his scars, the marks of crucifixion, the evidence of his suffering, the sign of what he had been through.

Does that seem odd to you? It seems odd to me. I'm continually surprised that the power of God that raised Jesus from the dead did not erase his scars. The joy of Easter morning did not blot out the marks of Jesus' journey through "the valley of the shadow of death." By the power of the Resurrection, the wounds had been healed, but the scars remained.

While I was working on this book, our journey through the liturgical year brought us to Christ the King Sunday, the last Sunday of the worship calendar, the day upon which the church celebrates the reign of Christ over the whole creation. In worship that day, we sang "Crown Him with Many Crowns." It's a familiar enough hymn; the words were imbedded in my memory from my childhood. But something happened within my soul when the congregation began to sing:

> Crown him the Lord of love;
> behold his hands and side,
> those wounds, yet visible above,
> in beauty glorified.
> All hail, Redeemer, hail!
> For thou hast died for me;
> thy praise and glory shall not fail
> throughout eternity.
> (*The United Methodist Hymnal*, United Methodist Publishing
> House, 1989, no. 327)

Unexpectedly, I was moved to tears. It was as if I could see the scars of those brutal, ugly, deadly wounds, still visible on the body of the Risen Christ, somehow, by the miraculous alchemy of grace, "in beauty glorified." And in some deep place in my own soul, I realized anew that those wounds were for me. The fresh awareness of it blew me away.

I love the simplicity of John's description of Jesus' appearance on that first Easter evening. (See John 20.) No thunder rolled and no lightning flashed. There were no blaring trumpets or beating drums; no mass choirs singing Handel's "Hallelujah" chorus; no white-robed Jesus being magically elevated from the tomb. In short, there was none of the theatrical pyrotechnics that have become the stock-in-trade of B-grade movies or megachurch Easter dramas. The Risen Christ comes quietly and simply stands among his close group of followers. It's like the unobtrusive way he joined those despairing disciples on the road to Emmaus, quietly walking along with them so that they did not realize who he was (see Luke 24:13-35). You have to love the gentle patience of a resurrected Lord who shows up like that!

In the upper room that night, Jesus spoke the words those fear-stricken disciples most deeply needed to hear, "Peace be with you" (John 20:19). Then he showed them the marks of the nails in his hands and feet, and the scar from the spear that had ripped open his side. Because of the scars, the disciples knew who he was.

We might as well tell the truth. It's one thing to believe in the Resurrection in worship on Easter Sunday morning, with the music and the crowds and the scent of lilies in the air. But it's something else to believe in the Resurrection in a post-Easter world. As hours turn into days and days turn into weeks, the Easter story can become little more than a pleasant memory of a fantastic dream. The extraordinary announcement that Jesus was raised from the dead can feel utterly unrelated to the messy, everyday stuff of our very messy, everyday lives. There are days when the gospel story seems just a little too good to be true; times when the Risen Christ seems too divine to have any connection with our mundane human experience.

I'm encouraged when I remember that faithful people have wrestled with the tension between the humanity and the divinity of Jesus since the earliest days of the Christian tradition. Some believed so strongly in the divinity of Jesus that they gave up on his humanity. They just couldn't handle a nail-scarred Christ.

The Gnostics (from the Greek word *gnosis*, meaning "knowledge") have gotten a lot of press in recent years because of the hype surrounding Dan Brown's fictional murder mystery *The Da Vinci*

Code, and the more scholarly publication of an ancient manuscript of *The Gospel of Judas.* The Gnostics believed in an absolute separation between the spiritual world, which was good, and the material world, which was evil. They believed that the goal of salvation is for the good spirit to escape the evil body in order to enter into a purely spiritual realm. In *The Gospel of Judas's,* for example, Jesus gives Judas the secret knowledge that Judas's action will liberate Jesus' spiritual self from his human body.

The Gnostics had no problem with the divinity of Jesus; it was his humanity they couldn't handle. They said that if Jesus was fully divine, he could not have been fully human. He must have been pretending. He must have been a divine spirit masquerading in human flesh. They could not believe in a Christ with scars.

The early Church declared Gnosticism to be heresy not because of what it affirmed about Jesus' divinity, but because of what it denied about his humanity. Gnosticism contradicted the shocking declaration that "the Word became flesh" (John 1:14)— real flesh and real blood—and that the Risen Christ had real scars to prove it.

Enter Thomas, forever identified as "Doubting Thomas" because it was so difficult for him to believe that the really human Jesus, who had really died, was now really alive.

Thomas wasn't there on that first Easter evening. He didn't experience the presence of the Risen Christ. He didn't see Jesus' hands and feet. He didn't hear the disciples returning from Emmaus describe the way their hearts burned within them when Jesus broke the bread and talked with them along the way. When Thomas finally showed up, the rest of the disciples expected him to believe in the Resurrection on the basis of their experience. But

Thomas was the spiritual ancestor of the founders of Missouri, the Show-Me State. He had to see the evidence for himself. He said, "Unless I see the mark of the nails on his hands, unless I put my finger into the place where the nails were, and my hand into his side, I will not believe" (John 20:25 NEB).

Days passed. The Gospel doesn't tell us what happened, but given the dubious track record of those first disciples, my guess is that as they moved farther away from that first Resurrection experience, some of the rest of them began questioning the Resurrection, too. Did they really see Jesus? Or was it just a projection of their inner desires? Did he really show them his scars? Or was that just a dream? And if it actually had happened, how would they explain it to anyone else? Why would anyone believe them? When they gathered together a week later, Thomas may not have been the only person in the room who had doubts about the reality of the Resurrection.

Again, it happened. Again, Jesus came and stood among them. Again, he said, "Peace be with you." Then he went directly to Thomas. He stretched out his hands and told Thomas, "Put your finger here and see my hands. Reach out your hand and put it in my side. Do not doubt but believe" (John 20:26-27).

Jesus showed Thomas his scars, the marks of his humanity, the symbol of the broken place in his life, and it was on the basis of those scars that Thomas realized who Jesus was.

As if the gospel story isn't strange enough, there's an even more peculiar twist in the text. Both Luke and John tell us that when the disciples saw Jesus' scars, they were filled with joy, although Luke does acknowledge that their joy was laced with disbelief. (See John 20:20 and Luke 24:41.)

That's odd to me. I doubt that my response to Jesus' scars would have been joy. If I had been there at the Crucifixion, if I had watched the blood flow from Jesus' hands, feet, and side, if I had seen his bloody, battered body being yanked down from the cross, if I had watched Joseph of Arimathea lay the corpse in his tomb, I think I would have wanted the Resurrection to erase all of the scars. I might have hoped for a superhuman Jesus who had been raised above human suffering and pain, in the hope that I might escape it, too. I might have preferred a Risen Christ who would wipe away any memory of the dark places in my life. I might have opted for a Gnostic, spiritualized Jesus who was totally separate from the ugly brokenness of the world so that I could be lifted above the messy, broken places in my life.

But John and Luke say that the disciples' response to Jesus' scars was joy. The scars let them know who Jesus was. His identity as the Risen Christ was defined by his identity as their crucified Lord. The signs of the world's victory over the way of Jesus became the sign of Jesus' victory over the ways of the world. If the cross was the ultimate sign of the world's power to break us, the Resurrection offers the hope that we can be made strong at the broken places, too.

After three decades of pastoral ministry, I've become convinced that Hemingway got it right when he said, "The world breaks everyone . . . the very good and the very gentle and the very brave impartially" (*A Farewell to Arms*, page 222). The Christian faith does not promise immunity from pain, suffering, defeat, or the sin of a broken world. I simply cannot find biblical or experiential evidence to support the claims of the "prosperity" preachers who promise that if we live by faith we will automatically become happy, rich, successful, pain-free, and good-looking.

But my experience also convinces me that Hemingway got it right when he said that "afterward many are strong at the broken places." It is precisely at the place where we are the most broken that we discover our most profound experience of the grace of God. It's only when we are willing to enter into our darkness that we discover the light.

I've seen a lot of people's scars, and not just the ones that are skin deep. I've seen the marks of what they've been through. They have taught me that joy can arise out of sorrow, that hope can be born out of pain, and that people who really know how to laugh are people who really know how to cry. They've taught me that the only way to find healing is to acknowledge our pain. The only way to experience grace is to confront our sin. The only place to find the light of new life is along the path that leads through the dark valley of the shadow of death. The only way to be made strong is to acknowledge where we are weak and to allow the God of grace to make us strong at those broken places.

I was scheduled to preach at Manning Road Methodist Church in Durban, South Africa, on the second Sunday after Easter. When the pastor asked for a text and sermon title, I told him I would preach on the story of the disciples on the Emmaus Road, because that would be the sermon I was going to preach to my own congregation before leaving the States.

I arrived in Durban less than an hour before the service was to begin. As I began to go over the Emmaus Road sermon, I began to have a deep sense that it simply did not fit the courageous people of that congregation who are attempting to become the healing presence of Christ in the brokenness of post-Apartheid South Africa. I kept thinking about a sermon I had preached sometime earlier on the risen and nail-scarred Christ, but try as I might, I could not bring it back into my mind.

When the pastor came to lead me to the sanctuary for the start of the service, I told him about the way I was struggling over the sermon. He remembered that my sermons are archived on our church's website. Within five minutes, we had gone to the site, printed off a copy of the earlier sermon, and were off to the service.

In worship that day, the young adults of Manning Road shared their witness of what the Spirit of God had done in their lives at their recent retreat. One by one, they talked about the way they had experienced the Risen Christ as they acknowledged some of the broken places in their lives and relationships. As I listened to their witness, I realized that they were bearing witness to the message I had just downloaded from the website. They had experienced the same peace that Jesus brought to those first disciples when he showed them his scars. By the time I got up to preach, I felt that the Risen Christ was already walking among us, showing us his scars, just the way he had been present to Thomas in the upper room.

One of my favorite pieces of classical music is the "Ode to Joy" from Beethoven's Ninth Symphony. Beethoven began thinking about it when he was twenty-five years old but kept laying it aside until the end of his life. That fact alone may suggest that we will never really understand joy until we experience some of the pain that life can throw at us. By the time he returned to the work, he was in poor health, burdened by the responsibility for a suicidal nephew, and completely deaf. At one point he wrote, "You can scarcely imagine how lonely and desperate my life has become."

But in that broken place of suffering silence he experienced a resurrection and wrote, "Despair will not overcome me. I will instead know joy, for how beautiful life is!" That's when he went to work on the "Ode to Joy."

Beethoven's now-familiar musical theme is first introduced by the low, somber strings, as if it is born in some deep, dark well of suffering in his soul. In response, the melody is picked up by the brighter, higher strings. Then it moves to the brass and begins to reverberate through the rest of the orchestra. A roaring tenor announces it as only a German tenor can. Finally, the chorus bursts into explosive, joyful sound. Beethoven reworks the theme over and over again as if to say that there are not enough ways to describe the kind of joy that emerges out of the deepest places of pain.

Beethoven's music became the familiar vehicle for Henry Van Dyke's words:

> Joyful, joyful we adore thee,
> God of glory, Lord of love;
> hearts unfold like flowers before thee,
> opening to the sun above.
> Melt the clouds of sin and sadness;
> drive the dark of doubt away.
> Giver of immortal gladness,
> fill us with the light of day.
> (*The United Methodist Hymnal*, no. 89)

Jesus, the fully divine and fully human Scar Lover, comes to stand among us. He shows us the scars in his hands and side. In those scars, we can find the grace that has the power to strengthen us in our broken places. In his risen presence we discover the power that can transform our dirge of sorrow into an ode to joy.

CHAPTER TWO

Sin: How Things Get Broken

Our sin is only and always that we put asunder what God has joined together.

—*William Sloane Coffin*, Letters to a Young Doubter

So, here's the question: How do things get broken, anyway? If the world breaks all of us, how did the breaking get started, and why does it keep happening?

In the late 1980s, author Robert Fulghum hit the bestseller list by declaring, "Everything I need to know I learned in kindergarten" in his book with that title. Based on that assumption, perhaps the best place to begin this chapter is with a familiar nursery rhyme that recounts the infamous tale of an unfortunate egg named Humpty Dumpty.

> Humpty Dumpty sat on a wall.
> Humpty Dumpty had a great fall.
> All the king's horses and all the king's men
> Couldn't put Humpty together again.

The nursery rhyme leaves some significant questions unanswered. How did an egg get up on the wall in the first place? An egg can't exactly roll up a wall by itself. Somebody must have put it there. Exactly why did he fall off the wall? Or is it *she*? *Humpty* is not exactly a gender-specific name. I'm sure that every personal injury attorney would ask if the builders of that wall had liability insurance. Was the wall built to the current building code? Were protective railings in place? Were notices posted that warned of the danger of falling off the wall? And perhaps the most practical question of all: Who is responsible for cleaning up the mess that Humpty Dumpty's fall left behind?

None of those questions are answered by Mother Goose, nor, as far as I can tell, by any of her successors in the nursery rhyme business. All we get is a yucky pile of shattered eggshell, floating around in a runny mess of egg whites and broken yolks that will start stinking if someone doesn't get busy cleaning it up.

Although he's been falling off the wall in one literary form or another since at least the early nineteenth century, you might ask how "Humpty Dumpty" ever made it into the nursery. It is, after all, a depressing little ditty that ends with no hope of Humpty Dumpty's being put back together again. In my most optimistic moments, I keep looking for another verse that no one remembers, like the forgotten verses of "The Star-Spangled Banner." But I looked it up. That's all there is; once on the wall, having had a great fall, all the human power available was incapable of putting that egg back together again.

It would be nothing more than a dismal English nursery rhyme, except for one thing: the Bible says that it's our story and that it happens to be true. The Creation narratives in Genesis say that we human beings were created, male and female, in the image of God. Talk about being non–gender-specific! The psalmist says that God made human beings just a little lower than the angels (see Psalm

8:5), which is a height that would have left Humpty Dumpty's head spinning.

The Bible also says that we took a great fall. It says that all of us have sinned and fallen short of the glory of God (see Romans 3:23). We're all good eggs who have fallen off the wall of God's loving, life-giving intention for us.

Eugene H. Peterson describes the reality we all can see when he writes, "Something is wrong here, dreadfully wrong. We feel it in our bones. . . . Creation is wonderful, but history is a mess" (*Christ Plays in Ten Thousand Places*, Eerdmans, 2005, pages 134, 136). Our world is littered with the eggshells of broken lives, broken promises, broken relationships, broken nations, broken hopes, broken dreams, and broken hearts. Sadly, the evidence is also that with all of our wisdom and all of our strength and all of our power and all of our might, we've never been able to put those pieces back together again.

The Bible has a word to describe the cause of all of the broken eggshells in our lives and our world. The Bible calls it *sin*.

President Calvin Coolidge had a reputation for being a man of few words. The story goes that he came home from church one day, and his wife, Grace, asked, "Was the sermon good?" The President said, "Yup." Grace asked, "What was it about?" "Sin," he said. She went on, "And what did the minister say?" President Coolidge replied, "He's against it."

If only it were that easy to deal with sin! But you know and I know that "Just Say No" just doesn't say enough. Sin is far more complicated, far more subtle than that. It lurks in the shadows of our souls. It hides in the dark corners of our relationships. It infects the murky complexity of the economic and political systems in the culture around us. It breaks our lives, our hearts, and our world and leaves scars on all of us. If we tell the truth, we all know that it takes more than just being against sin to deal with it.

In thinking about the way our world and our lives are broken by sin, I don't mean the petty little things that we often think of as "sins"—all the things our parents said we shouldn't do but which we go ahead and do anyway; the kind of things Catholics joke about confessing to their parish priest. The biblical view of sin is much bigger, broader, and deeper than that. The biblical writers describe a world in which the fault lines of sin have ruptured the order that the Creator intended, so that every part of our existence is in some sense knocked off its foundations, distorted in its vision, and out of sync with the Creator's purpose.

Augustine (A.D. 353–430) was one of the most notorious sinners to become a saint in Christian history. Looking back on his own journey, he remembered the time he and his young friends stole a few pears from a neighbor's orchard. The theft itself was a petty, small-scale "sin." What haunted Augustine's memory was not the theft itself, but the soul-level desire that lurked beneath it. He reflected on the theft in his *Confessions,* which stands as the classic work of spiritual autobiography.

> I was under no compulsion of need, unless a lack of moral sense can count as need, and a loathing for justice, and a greedy, full-fed love of sin. Yet I wanted to steal, and steal I did. I already had plenty of what I stole, and of much better quality too, and I had no desire to enjoy it when I resolved to steal it. I simply wanted to enjoy the theft for its own sake. . . . We derived pleasure from the deed simply because it was forbidden.

Augustine's soul-searching turned to prayer in which he described his own fall:

> O God, look upon this heart of mine, on which you took pity in its abysmal depths. Enable my heart to tell you now what it was seeking in this action which made me bad for no reason, in which there was no motive for my malice except malice. . . . I was in love with my own ruin, in love with decay: not with the thing for which I was falling into decay but with decay itself, for I was depraved in soul, and I leapt down from your strong support into destruction, hungering not for some advantage to be gained by the foul deed, but for the foulness itself.
>
> (*The Confessions*, Vintage Spiritual Classics, 1998, pages 30-31)

In our contemporary culture of self-affirmation, we might be tempted to say that Augustine suffered from a hyperactive conscience and that he poured the guilt on a bit thick. After all, it was just a few pears! But that would miss the point of his spiritual sensitivity and his insight into the human heart. His soul-level search for the reason he "leapt down" from the strong wall of God's goodness points us in the direction of the brokenness in all of our lives and in this creation.

In his insightful trilogy on "the powers," New Testament scholar Walter Wink describes the condition of our world in three fundamental affirmations: "The powers are good. The powers are fallen. The powers must be redeemed" (*Engaging the Powers*, Fortress, 1992, page 10). The biblical view of our human predicament is that, like Humpty Dumpty, we sat on a wall and had a great fall. But the gospel reverses the nursery rhyme's hopeless ending by announcing that by God's grace, we can be put together again. Our brokenness can be healed; our world can be redeemed.

Before opening the scars of some of the broken places in our lives, let me offer my own homegrown assumptions about sin.

First, sin breaks relationships. From a biblical perspective, sin is anything that disrupts, destroys, or damages our relationship with God, with ourselves, with others, and with the world around us. Sin is anything that shatters the wholeness of life that God intended from the first moments of creation. To paraphrase the traditional marriage vows, sin puts asunder that which God has put together.

If we are to begin to comprehend the broken places in our lives, we need to move beyond the idea of "sins" as often petty, sometimes insignificant, and usually self-oriented actions like Augustine's theft of the pears. The actions we define as "sins" are the surface-level cracks in the wall that reveal a seismic fault line deeper in the earth. It's as if Humpty Dumpty fell because the wall was sitting on the San Andreas Fault.

One of the formative experiences of my life and faith was hearing Archbishop Desmond Tutu address the World Methodist Conference in Nairobi, Kenya, in 1986. During some of the worst days of the struggle against Apartheid in South Africa, he declared that God created us "for togetherness, for community, for fellowship, for family, for interdependence."

Reflecting on the Creation narrative in Genesis, Archbishop Tutu said, "When God's will prevails fully, then all of his creation dwells in the harmony found in the beginning mythical times." In contrast to God's creative purpose, he said that "all kinds of things go horribly, badly wrong when we break this fundamental law of human existence" (*Proceedings of the Fifteenth World Methodist Conference*, World Methodist Council, 1987, pages 163-64).

The broken places in our lives are evidence of a deeper brokenness in our relationship with our Creator. We experience that brokenness either directly as a result of our own actions or indirectly as the result of the general brokenness of the world around us. But one thing is clear: sooner or later, a broken world breaks all of us. The fault lines tear apart our relationships with one another and our relationship with God.

Second, sin distorts goodness. In his classic *Mere Christianity*, C. S. Lewis said that "badness is only spoiled goodness." He said that sin is the pursuit of good things in the wrong ways and that we live in "a good world that has gone wrong, but still retains the memory of what it ought to have been" (*Mere Christianity*, Touchstone, 1996, pages 48-49). Saint Augustine defined evil as "the diminishment of good" (*The Confessions*, page 45). Thomas Merton called sin "the absence of a perfection that ought to be there. Sin as such is essentially boring because it is the lack of something that could appeal to our wills and our minds" (*A Thomas Merton Reader*, Image, 1989, page 66). The broken eggshells at the base of the wall keep reminding us of the original goodness that God intended.

William Sloane Coffin, who wrestled with sin the way Jacob wrestled with the angel, said, "Sins essentially represent freedom abused. . . . Sin is separation, a state of being in which we are alienated from God, from one another, and from our real and loving selves. Sin is rending the bond of love, and its punishment is experiencing the bond of love rent" (*Letters to a Young Doubter*, pages 81-82).

I can still hear the elf-like laughter in Archbishop Tutu's voice when he described God looking out on creation "in divine delight, rubbing his hands in approval, that it was not just good, but that it was all *very* good" (italics his). He went on to describe what happened when Adam and Eve sinned: "Their spiritual condition had deleterious consequences for the material universe. The earth brought forth thistles . . . enmity ensued between the humans and the rest of the animal creation. Nature became red in tooth and claw" (*Proceedings of the Fifteenth World Methodist Conference,* page 164).

Vice is the inversion of virtue. A healthy desire for food is reduced to gluttony; the longing for love is twisted into lust; the need for rest degenerates into sloth; healthy self-respect metastasizes into arrogant pride; patriotism devolves into jingoistic nationalism. The broken places in our lives are a result of the twisting of a God-given desire to a selfish end. It is turning away from the life-giving purpose of God toward something that corrupts and pollutes the goodness of our lives and of the created order.

Third, sin is deadly. Because it breaks relationships and because it distorts goodness, sin always results in some kind of death—the death of the life, love, health, and joy that God intends for our lives and for the whole creation. The wages of sin are always death (see Romans 6:23). Eugene Peterson concludes that "death provides the fundamental datum that something isn't working the way it was intended, accompanied by the feeling that we have every right to expect something other and better" (*Christ Plays in Ten Thousand Places,* page 137).

In the hillside cemetery in Clarion, Pennsylvania, where my paternal forebears are buried, a gravestone marks the resting place of John Harold Harnish, born on June 4, 1916. He was my grandparents' firstborn son.

Harold died on November 4, 1918, a toddler victim of the flu pandemic that swept across the country in the aftermath of "the

Great War," known today as World War I. Somewhere between 20 million and 100 million people worldwide lost their lives in what has been called the most devastating epidemic in history, although the AIDS pandemic has a good chance of replacing it. An estimated 675,000 Americans died of the 1918 flu pandemic, ten times as many as died in the war. It was particularly deadly for the very young and the very old.

Historians and medical scholars have debated the specific causes for the pandemic, naming everything from the filth of the trenches and mustard gas attacks on the battlefield, to the greed of pharmaceutical companies that encouraged the use of untested vaccines to generate corporate profits. Most agree that the spread of the virus was a byproduct of the seismic shifting of people and infections that resulted from the war itself. Even the Armistice Day celebrations, with their massive parades and parties, helped spread the virus through American cities, becoming what one authority called "a complete disaster from the public health standpoint" (http://virus.stanford.edu/uda/).

Harold, like so many other innocent children, died as the indirect victim of a war he was far too young to fight. The sin of global conflict between nations resulted in massive, innocent death. And it continues today. Even as I write, a Johns Hopkins University study estimates that as many as 650,000 civilians have died in Iraq since the launching of a war that began for dubious reasons and that, at the time of this writing, seems to have no end.

Fourth, sin can be redeemed. The good news is that the God of creation is also the God of redemption. The Bible is the story of the lengths to which a loving God would go to mend, heal, and redeem a sin-broken creation.

The biblical label to describe God's work of healing in this broken creation is "salvation." It comes from the same Greek root as the word *healing*. The God who first breathed life into creation is eternally opposed to anything that destroys, demeans, or distorts the goodness of the creation, or that cheapens or abuses life. The bold affirmation of the Christian gospel is that all of the power of an infinitely loving God is determined to do everything that God can do—even if it means going to a cross—to put things back together again, to restore wholeness, to heal our broken lives, and to renew the harmony that God has always intended. According to Eugene Peterson, salvation is not "a last ditch effort to salvage a few planks and timbers from a wrecked ship." Rather, it is God's "main business in history" (*Christ Plays in Ten Thousand Places*, page 148).

Dramatist Eugene O'Neill wrestled with this theme in his play "The Great God Brown." In the closing scene, his main character says, "This is Daddy's bedtime secret for today: Man is born broken. He lives by mending. The grace of God is glue!" (*The Plays of Eugene O'Neill*, Random House, 1954, page 318). The utterly unmerited, undeserved, unearned grace of God is the power by which God is at work to save, redeem, and restore our broken lives and this broken creation.

In his letter to the Corinthians, the apostle Paul used the word *reconciliation* to describe the saving work of God. It literally means bringing things that have been separated back together to create agreement and harmony.

> For the love of Christ urges us on, because we are convinced that one has died for all; therefore all have died. And he died for all,

so that those who live might live no longer for themselves, but for him who died and was raised for them. From now on, therefore, we regard no one from a human point of view; even though we once knew Christ from a human point of view, we know him no longer in that way. So if anyone is in Christ, there is a new creation: everything old has passed away; see, everything has become new! All this is from God, who reconciled us to himself through Christ, and has given us the ministry of reconciliation; that is, in Christ God was reconciling the world to himself, not counting their trespasses against them, and entrusting the message of reconciliation to us. (2 Corinthians 5:14-19)

Charles Wesley put that text to song in his hymn "Arise, My Soul, Arise."

Arise, my soul, arise; shake off thy guilty fears;
The bleeding sacrifice in my behalf appears:
Before the throne my surety stands,
Before the throne my surety stands,
My name is written on His hands.

My God is reconciled; His pardoning voice I hear;
He owns me for His child; I can no longer fear:
With confidence I now draw nigh,
With confidence I now draw nigh,
And "Father, Abba, Father," cry.
(*Hymns and Sacred Poems*, 1742)

Confronting the evil of Apartheid at a time when it seemed to be immovably entrenched in his homeland, Archbishop Desmond Tutu concluded his address to the World Methodist Conference with the exuberant declaration of his confidence in God's work of redemption:

Praise be to God that our God is a God who enlists us, all of us, to be fellow workers with him, to extend his kingdom of righteousness, to help change the ugliness of this world—its hatred, its enmity, its poverty, its disease, its alienation, its anxiety. He enlists us to be fellow workers with him, to transfigure it into the laughter and the joy, the compassion and the goodness, the love and the peace, the justice and the reconciliation of his kingdom as we work with him to make the kingdoms of this world to become the kingdom of our God and of his Christ.

And, hey, victory is assured! Because the death and resurrection of our Savior Jesus Christ declares forever and ever that light has overcome darkness, that life has overcome death, that joy and laughter and peace and compassion and justice and caring and sharing, all and more have overcome their counterparts. (*Proceedings of the Fifteenth World Methodist Conference*, pages 168-69)

If Humpty Dumpty is the story of the way things get broken, the gospel is the story of the way God puts things back together again. And that includes every broken one of us!

CHAPTER THREE

Temptation: Where the Wild Things Are

Our life in this world is tempting because it accommodates us to its order. . . . A disordered fastening on lowest goods makes us fall from higher goods, from the highest of all, you my God, my lord, your truth, your law.

—Saint Augustine, quoted in Gary Wills, St. Augustine

Parents of young children, elementary school teachers, and adults of a certain age will recognize the title of this chapter as a direct rip-off of the title of the award-winning children's book by Maurice Sendak (*Where the Wild Things Are,* Harper Trophy, 1963, pages unnumbered).

Sendak tells the story of Max, who wore his wolf suit and made so much mischief around the house that his mother called him "Wild Thing" and sent him to bed without his supper. That night, Max's room became a forest from which Max sailed off in his imagination to "the place where the wild things are." The wild things "roared their terrible roars and gnashed their terrible teeth and rolled their terrible eyes and showed their terrible claws."

But Max said, "Be still!" and stared "into all their yellow eyes without blinking once and they were frightened and called him the most wild thing of all." The wild things made him their king and there was a wild rumpus, until Max discovered that "he was lonely and wanted to be where someone loved him best of all." He left the wild things behind and sailed back to "his very own room where he found his supper waiting for him and it was still hot."

I wouldn't begin to suggest that Sendak had the New Testament in mind when he wrote his children's book. But Matthew, Mark, and Luke all agree that the critical turning point in Jesus' life was his journey into the wilderness of temptation where, according to Mark, "he was with the wild beasts" (Mark 1:13).

Physically speaking, Max's journey took him no farther than his bedroom. In the same sense, we need not attempt to locate the wilderness where Jesus faced temptation on a desert terrain of ancient Palestine. Throughout the Bible, the wilderness is more than just a place on the map; it is a place in the soul. It's that deep, inner place where we wrestle with the most basic issues of our identity. It's the place where we uncover the scars that life has left upon us and make critical decisions about who we are and where we are going in the light of who God is calling us to be.

A couple of years ago our worship planning team invited the people of our congregation to complete this sentence: "I've always wanted to hear a sermon on . . ." As you might expect, some of the most interesting responses were also anonymous.

One said, "I've always wanted to hear a sermon on jealousy, lust, envy, dealing with Satan in the daily world." That sounded like a person who was facing a lot of wild beasts in his or her life. Another wrote, "I've always wanted to hear a sermon on how to keep faith during the trials of life." At first glance, it looked like the person had written, "How to keep *fit* during the trials of life," which would not be bad, either. Looking the wild beasts of temptation in the eye without blinking takes all the spiritual fitness we can muster. Another said, "I've always wanted to hear a sermon on the ways we sin in small things."

The people who wrote those words know how it feels to be in the wilderness. They've confronted the wild beasts of temptation. They have faced up to what Charles Wesley called "our bent to sinning," the interior forces that entice us to settle for less than God's best for us.

When Matthew and Luke tell the wilderness story, they name the specific temptations Jesus faced, but Mark doesn't do that. In a sense, Mark leaves it up to us to fill in the blanks, which is probably okay because temptation is always an intensely personal matter. The very thing that seems like a wild beast for me may be a tame kitten to you. But we all face them. Sooner or later, we all are broken by them. So, what are those temptations for you? What is the adversary you face? Where do you wrestle with the power of Satan? What are the wild things in your life?

In the biblical tradition, the journey toward redemption always goes through the wilderness where we wrestle with the wild beasts in our own experience. Just the way Sendak's Max stared into the eyes of the wild things without blinking, we are called to look temptation in the eye, to name it, and to face it, the way Jesus faced it in the wilderness.

Have you ever wondered how these temptation stories made it into the Gospels? It's clear that Jesus was alone in the wilderness. It's not as if the desert caves were bugged or CNN had planted a hidden camera out there. The only way this story could have been passed down to us would be for Jesus to have shared it. Just the way the Risen Christ showed them the scars on his hands and side, Jesus must have opened this dark, inner struggle to his disciples, allowing them to enter into the wilderness experience with him, allowing them to find strength to confront their temptations the way he confronted his.

In the wilderness, Jesus teaches us to remember who we are. In Matthew's account, two of the three temptations begin with the words, "If you are the Son of God . . ." (see Matthew 4:3-7). The Greek text could also be translated, "Because you are the Son of God."

It's no accident that Matthew places this story immediately following Jesus' baptism, when Jesus heard a voice from heaven saying, "You are my Son, the Beloved, in whom I am well pleased" (Matthew 3:17, paraphrased). The basic temptation Jesus faced was to believe a lie about his own identity. The devil tempted him to use his identity as the Son of God for a selfish purpose rather than for the saving purpose of God. But, as the old country proverb says, "A lie may carry you far, but it will never carry you home." Jesus knew that being the Son of God meant being faithful to God's purpose. He remembered who he was. And in the struggle with our own wild beasts, it helps to be reminded of who we are: sons and daughters of God.

In 1733, John Wesley released his first published work, *A Collection of Forms of Prayer for Every Day of the Week.* Wesley said that prayer begins with "a thorough conviction that we are God's; that He is the proprietor of all we are, and all we have; and that not only by right of creation, but of purchase; for He died for all." The result of that fundamental affirmation of our identity in Christ results in a passionate desire "to live unto God; to render unto God the things which are God's, even all we are, and all we have;

to glorify Him in our bodies, and in our spirits, with all the power and all the strength of each; and to make his will our sole principle of action" (*John and Charles Wesley: Selected Writings and Hymns*, Paulist Press, 1981, page 78).

I have a friend who placed a simple plaque on the wall next to the door that led from the kitchen to the garage—the door through which every member of the family would leave as they went to work or school each day. The plaque simply read, "Remember who you are." They went out to face their daily temptations with the reminder that they were sons and daughters of God, marked by the watery sign of baptism and claimed by the Holy Spirit.

In the wilderness Jesus teaches us to live in the Word. Jesus found strength to confront temptation through the written words of scripture. In Matthew's account, Jesus responds to every temptation by drawing on his memory of scripture.

To be sure, the devil quotes scripture, too, twisting it to serve his own purpose, and we are capable of doing that, too. It's frighteningly easy for us to read scripture looking for how we can use it, rather than watching for the way it might use us. But Jesus counters every temptation with the words of scripture that were planted deep in his soul.

There is a monument in memory of the Reverend Dr. Martin Luther King, Jr., in one of the towns where he marched in the challenging days of the Civil Rights Movement. Engraved upon it are the words, "Let justice roll down like waters . . ." Beneath the quotation is Dr. King's name, giving the impression that those are his words. But Dr. King knew that they were not his words. They are the words of the Old Testament prophet Amos: "Let justice roll down like waters, / and righteousness like an everflowing stream"

(Amos 5:24). They became Dr. King's words because his sermons and speeches were saturated with both direct references and indirect allusions to scripture. His mind and heart were so deeply soaked in scripture that the words of scripture became his own. He did not speak on his own authority, but he drew on the authority of the written word.

In quoting Amos, Dr. King knew that biblical "justice" is more than judgment or retribution. It is not just getting our pound of flesh out of the person who has done evil against us, which seems to be the way the word has been used in recent times.

While the biblical vision of justice contains the element of judgment, it is much larger and more positive than that. Biblical justice is defined by God's special concern for the poor, the powerless, and the oppressed. It describes God's vision of a world in which all people have enough and all of God's children receive their just share of the world's bounty. It is the expression of God's intention that every human being be treated with the dignity and respect that they deserve as children of God. When Dr. King drew on the words of Amos, he was bringing that biblical heritage to bear on the conditions of injustice he saw in our nation. It was the product of a life that was soaked in scripture.

In his "Advice on Spiritual Reading," John Wesley instructed his followers to "select also any remarkable saying or advices, and treasure them up in your memory; that these you may either draw forth in time of need, as arrows from a quiver, against temptation (more especially against the solicitations to that sin which most easily besets you) or make use of as incitements to any virtue, to humility, patience, or the love of God" (*John and Charles Wesley: Selected Writings and Hymns*, page 89).

The writer of the epistle of James challenged his readers to "welcome with meekness the implanted word that has the power to save your souls" (James 1:21). I like that phrase—"the implanted word." I've discovered that one of the ways to overcome temptation is to draw on the deep roots of faith and strength that are available to us when the words of scripture are planted deep within our hearts and minds.

In the wilderness Jesus teaches us to remember that we are not alone. Both Matthew and Mark record that at the end of the temptation, angels came and waited on Jesus (see Matthew 4:11; Mark 1:13). The verb they used literally means "to wait at table." It conjures up for me the imagery of those familiar words in the Twenty-third Psalm, "Thou preparest a table before me in the presence of my enemies" (RSV).

To tell you the truth, "in the presence of my enemies" is not where I'd prefer to have my table prepared! I'd prefer to have my table set in the "green pastures" or "beside still waters" (Psalm 23:2). But that's not what the psalmist said. The table is set in the presence of our enemies, just the way the table where the angels waited on Jesus was in the wilderness. And that's where the angels will set *our* table, too.

The Southern novelist Flannery O'Connor said that her subject in fiction was "the action of grace in territory held largely by the devil" (*Mystery and Manners*, page 118, cited at www.georgetown .edu/faculty/bassr/heath/syllabuild/iguide/oconnor.html). The grace that leads toward the mending of the broken places in our lives meets us in territory largely held by the devil. There are wild beasts there, sure enough, but there are angels, too, who will help us find our way back home.

One of the formative influences in the life of John Wesley was his experience with a group of Moravian Christians on his way back to England after his ill-fated missionary work in Georgia. He translated thirty-three of their German hymns into English. One of those hymns captures the struggle most of us face with temptation:

> Thy secret voice invites me still
> > The sweetness of thy yoke to prove;
> And fain I would: but though my will
> > Be fix'd, yet wide my passions rove.
> Yet hindrances strew all the way;
> I aim at thee, yet from thee stray.

If most of us are honest with ourselves, we know the internal wrestling those words describe. In that struggle, the hymnist prayed

> O Love, thy sovereign aid impart,
> > To save me from low-thoughted care:
> Chase this self-will through all my heart,
> > Through all its latent mazes there.
>
> . . . .
>
> To feel thy power, to hear thy voice,
> To taste thy love is all my choice.

(*John and Charles Wesley: Selected Writings and Hymns,* pages 90-91)

Whatever else Matthew and Mark mean when they refer to "angels," I take it to mean that in the end, the power of God's grace was available to strengthen Jesus in his temptation.

People who honor the ministry of Mother Teresa may be surprised to discover that it took more than a year for her spiritual leaders to affirm God's call for her to leave the convent and go to serve the poorest of India's poor. Even then, the early days of what became The Missionaries of Charity were fraught with such profound challenges that Mother Teresa referred to it as "the dark night of the birth of the Society." She prayed, "May God give me courage now—this moment—to persevere in following your call."

Like Jesus in the wilderness, Mother Teresa faced the temptation to find an easier way to fulfill her calling. Once when her legs were exhausted from walking the streets of Calcutta, she wrote that "the temptation grew strong" to return to the community at Loreto. She recounted "all the beautiful things and comforts—the people they mix with—in a word everything" that awaited her there. She prayed, "Today—my God—what tortures of loneliness. . . . My God, give me courage now to fight self and the temper. Let me not draw back from the sacrifice I have made of my free choice and conviction." Her biographer sounded a lot like Matthew or Mark describing the way the angels strengthened Jesus when he wrote, "Her ability to bear the pain and loneliness had now reached her limit. Certain that by her own strength she could not cope, she turned to God in prayer." In the life of prayer, she found the strength to go on (*Come Be My Light,* Doubleday, 2007, pages 133-36).

The good news is that the same power that strengthened Jesus in the wilderness is available to each of us.

Sometimes that power comes directly through the memory of the written word.

Sometimes that power comes through the spiritual discipline of prayer.

Sometimes that power comes through in-depth counseling or therapy to deal with our addictions, damaged memories of the past, or early conditioning in our lives.

Sometimes it comes through a decisive change of patterns and practices of our lives.

Often that power comes through the community of faith in which brothers and sisters listen to us, support us in our struggles, and hold us accountable for our choices.

God's power can come in a variety of ways, but the promise is that the same angels who waited on Jesus in the wilderness are present and waiting on us when we wrestle with the wild beasts of temptation.

Martin Luther, who knew what it meant to wrestle with the powers of darkness in his own life, captured the assurance of God's power at work within us in the hymn that energized the Protestant Reformation:

> Did we in our own strength confide,
> our striving would be losing,
> were not the right man on our side,
> the man of God's own choosing.
> Dost ask who that may be?
> Christ Jesus, it is he;
> Lord Sabaoth, his name,
> from age to age the same,
> and he must win the battle.
>
> And though this world, with devils filled,
> should threaten to undo us,
> we will not fear, for God hath willed
> his truth to triumph through us.

The Prince of Darkness grim,
we tremble not for him;
his rage we can endure,
for lo, his doom is sure;
one little word shall fell him.
("A Mighty Fortess Is Our God," *The United Methodist Hymnal*,
no. 110)

When the temptations were over, Jesus returned to his hometown to begin his ministry. Luke records, "When the devil had finished every test, he departed from him until an opportune time" (Luke 4:13). The wild beasts would come again, just as they will come again for us. But like Max in Maurice Sendak's book, we know that there is a place where we can return to the One who loves us best of all. The place where supper is waiting, a table is prepared, and our heavenly Father will welcome us home.

CHAPTER FOUR
Lust: Taming the Fatal Attraction

*What you tell me about in the nights. That is not love. That is
only passion and lust. When you love, you wish to do things for.
You wish to sacrifice for. You wish to serve.*

—*Ernest Hemingway,* A Farewell to Arms

Orson Welles, whose radio voice became familiar across the
nation as Lamont Cranston ("The Shadow knows!"), described
what happened the first time he tried to commit adultery. He said
that the romantic atmosphere was suddenly broken when he heard
his own voice on the hotel room radio, asking the all-too-
appropriate question, "Who knows what evil lurks in the hearts of
men?" (*Time,* October 7, 1985, page 70). The evil that lurks in many
of our hearts, the place where the world breaks many of us, is the
broken place called lust.

It's easy for a preacher to rail against the pervasive influence of
lust in our culture today, from Janet Jackson's "wardrobe malfunc-
tion" to *Desperate Housewives,* from the gratuitous sexuality of television advertising to the invasive availability and addictive power
of Internet pornography. The problem with that approach is that all
of us good, churchgoing people can go on pretending that the problem is "out there" rather than "in here." We can go away shaking

our fingers in self-righteous indignation at the world without facing up to the broken places in ourselves. It only goes to prove that "denial is more than a river in Egypt."

I was finishing the first draft of this book when the newspapers and television stations reported that a pastor I know was taking a leave of absence from ministry because of his addiction to Internet pornography. The news struck me on several levels. I have known this guy since he was a kid. I had watched from a distance as he gave leadership to a rapidly growing congregation. I knew that he is a very good guy, a good husband and father, and a good pastor with a Christ-centered heart and a genuine commitment to ministry. I knew that if it could happen to him, it could happen to any of us.

We can, of course, *lust* for just about anything—power, success, wealth, pleasure—but most of the time when most of us hear the word, we associate it with sexual desire, which is certainly the case in our contemporary culture. So, let's think about lust as the dark side of love. If sin is spoiled goodness, then lust is rotten love. Whereas love is self-sharing, lust is self-gratification. Lust is sexual desire without a loving relationship. It is using another person to satisfy our own sexual needs with little or no interest in meeting the needs of the other person.

Looking back on what he described as "the mud of my fleshly desires," Augustine said, "I could not distinguish the calm light of love from the fog of lust" (*The Confessions*, page 24). That same confusion permeates the culture around us. Here are a few examples.

I pulled into the grocery store parking lot behind a pickup truck with a Texas license plate and a bumper sticker that announced, "Cowboy butts just drive me nuts." You don't have to be from Texas to know lust when you see it!

A ruthlessly honest friend confessed, "I don't need to know someone's name to lust after them." And that's precisely the point: lust is sexual desire that doesn't need to know the other person's name.

I've never quite figured out why the news media thought it was such a big deal for President Jimmy Carter to acknowledge that he had lusted after women in his heart. It simply meant that he knew his Bible better than they did, and that he was a whole lot like the rest of us.

The tagline for the Oscar-nominated movie *Brokeback Mountain* declared that "love is a force of nature." That's almost as silly as the 1970s movie blockbuster *Love Story*, which announced, "Love means never having to say you're sorry."

Lust is a force of nature. It's a natural, God-given desire that can be good or bad, healthy or destructive, depending on what we do with it. But *love* is something else. Love is more than just the satisfaction of a natural desire or passion. Love is a way of living in relationship that determines what we do with our natural, God-given, but sin-infected desires. A "force of nature" is an animal instinct that functions without conscious thought. Love—particularly the love of God defined in the words, way, and will of Jesus—involves a choice to give itself for the sake of another.

One biblical example of the difference between lust and love might be Matthew's description of Joseph. He's the man in the shadows of the birth narratives; the character without any lines in the Christmas pageant. But here's what love looked like for Joseph: "He did as the angel of the Lord commanded him; he took her as his wife, but had no marital relations with her until she had borne a son" (Matthew 1:24-25). Not much "force of nature" there!

For Joseph, love meant making a radical choice to deny his own desires for the sake of the one he loved.

The Bible never hesitates to remove the carefully placed bandages we use to cover over the scars of lust. The most dramatic example is the R-rated story that marks the turning point in the life of David. It's recorded in 2 Samuel 11–12. It begins on a sunlit spring afternoon, when David looked out over his balcony and noticed a beautiful woman bathing in the courtyard below. At this point in the story, David did not even know her name. All he knew was that he wanted her for himself. He brought her to his chamber, had intercourse with her, and sent her home.

But life is never that simple. Bathsheba announced that she was pregnant. What began with David's springtime afternoon of lust devolved into the lies and murder of his attempted cover-up and resulted in the death of their child, the wreckage of David's dysfunctional family, and ultimately the sad end of David's reign. The biblical storytellers were sure that the decline began when David looked out from his porch, saw a woman taking a bath, observed that she was beautiful, and acted on "a force of nature."

There is, of course, a movie version of this biblical story, implied by the title of this chapter. It was the 1987 blockbuster *Fatal Attraction*. When it was released, one reviewer called it "a homily for our times." The movie was even more lurid and lustful, more brutal and bloody than the story of David. But it did convince a whole lot of biblically illiterate folks in my generation of the biblical truth that David's story demonstrates, namely that there are unexpected and often deadly consequences to our lustful actions.

But the Bible doesn't leave the story where our human stories of lust usually end. It offers a word of grace for that broken place in our lives and relationships. David found that grace when he prayed,

> Have mercy on me, O God,
>   according to your steadfast love;
> according to your abundant mercy
>   blot out my transgressions.
> Wash me thoroughly from my iniquity,
>   and cleanse me from my sin.
>
> For I know my transgressions,
>   and my sin is ever before me.
>
> . . . .
>
> Purge me with hyssop, and I shall be clean;
>   wash me, and I shall be whiter than snow.
> Let me hear joy and gladness;
>   let the bones that you have crushed rejoice.
> Hide your face from my sins,
>   and blot out all my iniquities.
>
> Create in me a clean heart, O God,
>   and put a new and right spirit within me.
>
> . . . .
>
> Restore to me the joy of your salvation,
>   and sustain in me a willing spirit.
> (Psalm 51:1-3, 7-10, 12)

The gospel story of God's grace in the broken place of lust is recorded in the eighth chapter of the Gospel of John. The self-righteous religious rulers brought a woman to Jesus who had been caught in the act of adultery. I've always wondered exactly what these frighteningly pious people were doing when they found her and what they did with her companion. They found her nonetheless, and they made her stand there in front of Jesus in the naked humiliation of her sin, demanding that she be stoned, just the way the law required.

John says that Jesus "bent down and wrote with his finger on the ground." Preachers have long attempted to make their own guess at what Jesus wrote in the dust that day. I don't think it matters. If it mattered, the Gospel writer would have told us. My guess is that it was a lot like the way we drop our head and drag our toe around in the sand when we are embarrassed, unwilling to look the people around us in the eye. Perhaps Jesus was trying to deflect attention away from the woman's humiliation and shame. Finally, he looked up and said, "Let anyone among you who is without sin be the first to throw a stone at her." Then he bent down and went back to writing in the sand. There must have been a long, uncomfortable silence before they all turned and went away and Jesus was left alone with this obviously guilty woman.

Jesus looked up and asked, "Woman, where are they? Has no one condemned you?" She replied, "No one, sir." And then Jesus spoke what had to be the most beautiful words she had ever heard, "Neither do I condemn you. Go your way, and from now on do not sin again" (John 8:2-11).

The one person on the planet who was without sin, the one person who had the right to condemn this woman, pardoned her and sent her off to live a new life. John concludes the story with Jesus saying, "I am the light of the world. Whoever follows me will never walk in darkness but will have the light of life" (John 8:12).

Did you notice what Jesus did for the woman? First, he forgave her. My sense is that many of us who struggle with the power of lust are already feeling the burden of guilt or shame. I can't find any evidence that condemnation is very helpful, except to the person who does the condemning or, at best, as a powerful way in which the Spirit of God motivates us for change. What is needed is not condemnation, but forgiveness, pardon, the grace of God that meets us in the dark places of our lives with the good news, "Neither do I condemn you."

Jesus loves us just the way we are, but he loves us too much to leave us the way we are. He sent the woman into a new way of life when he said, "Go and sin no more." In addition to pardon, he offers power—his power, the power of the Holy Spirit of God to go and live a new, clean life. The good news for every one of us lost and lustful sinners is that God's grace offers us pardon for our sin and power to live a new life.

In his first letter to the Thessalonians, Paul describes both God's call to a life of holiness and God's power that is available to strengthen us to live it:

> It is God's will that you should . . . avoid sexual immorality; that each of you should learn to control his own body in a way that is holy and honorable, not in passionate lust like the heathen, who do not know God. . . . For God did not call us to be impure, but to live a holy life. (1 Thessalonians 4:3-5, 7 NIV)

> May [the Spirit] strengthen your hearts so that you will be blameless and holy in the presence of our God and Father when our Lord Jesus comes with all his holy ones. (1 Thessalonians 3:13 NIV)

With this biblical background, let me offer some practical steps along the way toward the discovery of grace for the dark place of lust in our lives.

1. Get honest. Tell the truth, if not to someone else, at least to yourself. It's amazing how things that seem powerful in the darkness lose some of their power when they are brought into the light. The biblical word for that is to *confess* it, to acknowledge the reality of our sin and our need of God's grace. The process is like that of the twelve steps of Alcoholics Anonymous, which call for "a ruthless moral inventory," in which we name our sin and ask for forgiveness.

2. Get forgiven. Receive the undeserved forgiveness and grace of God. Read again David's prayer of repentance and forgiveness (see Psalm 51). Like him, and like the woman caught in adultery, the forgiveness and cleansing grace of God are available for each of us. The process may also involve asking for forgiveness from a person we have hurt or offended.

3. Get help. If lust has led you into some form of sexual addiction, you'll never get free of it by yourself. It's like getting out of quicksand. You'll need a trained therapist or counselor, or at least the help of a trusted Christian friend to get you through. Don't try to do this on your own. Just the way sin separates us from one another, grace draws us into Christian community where we find strength from one another.

4. Get smart. Wise up. Martin Luther supposedly said that you can't keep the birds of temptation from flying over your head, but you don't need to help them build a nest in your hair. How different David's story would be if, when he saw Bathsheba taking her bath, he had simply gone inside and taken a cold shower!

I know a businessman who travels around the country in his work. That means that he spends a lot of nights alone in hotel rooms, many of which have an abundant supply of pornography available at the touch of a button on the remote. This man told me that he broke his addiction to video pornography by taking along a picture of his wife and kids. When he gets to the hotel room, he places it right beside the television, as a reminder of the people who love him and the people he loves. His love for them is stronger than his lust for pornography.

5. *Get healed.* If lust is the inversion of love, then healing comes in discovering the love that God intended for you to share. The journey may be long and hard, but the promise of the gospel is that you can learn to love and be loved in the way God intended.

Rummaging around in my files, I found an unsigned letter that I received many years ago. I kept it because it is a powerful witness of both the destructive power of lust and the redeeming power of grace.

> Our marriage suffered a severe trauma. . . . We have struggled to re-establish the kind of trust and security between us that we thought was there. We have come to know the true meaning of suffering, confusion, shame, and forgiveness. We have experienced the limits of reason and have known the terror of walking that ledge between insanity and depression. We have sought understanding through individual and family therapists, through long discussions with friends who have suffered similarly, and by making a commitment to search for answers through an examination of our faith. For me, it has been a long walk, not just with Jesus, but with the demons of my childhood, the terrifying remembrance of a war too painful to examine, and an admission

of my futile attempt to live an unexamined, secretive life where there were no boundaries, no accountability, no standards. . . . When I emerged from that fog, bloody and bruised, I saw the truth . . . that it wasn't just me that I had sacrificed . . . that others, especially my wife, had taken every blow and suffered every indignity I had created for myself.

It's been a long walk, yet we have taken it. We have come to discover that our love is immense and, although tentative at times, tenacious. We are hopeful and appreciative and excited and joyful and scared and determined and committed. Committed to each other . . . committed to the belief that I can live again within the boundaries of our vows . . . committed to the understanding that, by bringing God into our lives, we can face any situation, endure any tragedy, experience joy beyond reason, and make a difference in the lives of others.

Only the grace of God can do that! It's the grace that meets us with healing for our hurts, and strength for the broken places of our lives and relationships.

CHAPTER FIVE

Greed and Envy: When Enough Isn't Enough

Possessions are not God's blessing and goodness, but the opportunities of service which God entrusts to us.

—*Dietrich Bonhoeffer,* The Cost of Moral Leadership

What would you be willing to do for $10 million? Several years ago a nationwide survey revealed some surprising answers to that question. A shocking percentage of people were ready and willing to abandon their families, become prostitutes for a week, leave their spouses, or give up their United States citizenship for the money.

What are you willing to do for money? How much of your integrity will you give away for greed? How much of your character will you sell off for wealth? Is the way we use our money consistent with our commitment to Christ?

The invitation of this book is for each of us to acknowledge our scars and to confront some of the broken places in our lives; to track down the sneaky culprit of sin and to discover the way the grace of God, revealed at the cross, can meet us in those dark places and lead us into the life and light of resurrection.

One of the diagnostic tools for exploring the broken places in our lives comes down to us from the sixth century, in what Pope Gregory named The Seven Deadly Sins. In the last chapter we looked at lust, the sin that the entertainment world often treats as a joke. In this chapter we turn to the sibling sins of greed and envy, which sometimes turn out to be the way the world defines success. This attitude was given classic expression in the 1987 movie *Wall Street*, when Gordon Gekko (played by Michael Douglas) said:

> The point is, ladies and gentleman, that greed—for lack of a better word—is good. Greed is right. Greed works. Greed clarifies, cuts through, and captures the essence of the evolutionary spirit. Greed, in all of its forms—greed for life, for money, for love, knowledge—has marked the upward surge of mankind. And greed—you mark my words—will not only save Teldar Paper, but that other malfunctioning corporation called the USA. (www.americanrhetoric .com/MovieSpeeches/moviespeechwallstreet.html)

Well, let's see what Jesus has to say about that. The story recorded in Luke 12:13-34 begins with a very practical request from a man in the crowd. "Teacher," he said, "tell my brother to divide the family inheritance with me."

It's a practical dilemma. Every local church's planned-giving committee would be quick to point out that this is what happens when people don't have a will or an estate plan. It leaves the kids with a mess.

In this case, because of the common laws of primogeniture, the elder brother evidently got the whole estate, leaving this younger brother out. As is often the case, dividing the estate had divided the family. So, this man came to Jesus as a teacher, a rabbi, an authority in the law, as one who represented a just sharing of resources, to ask him to help sort it out.

Jesus avoids taking sides in this particular family squabble, as if to say, "Sorting out estates is not my job. What you need is a good lawyer." But the implied greed of the elder brother and the suggested envy of the younger brother created the setting for Jesus' warning in verse 15: "Take care! Be on your guard against all kinds of greed; for one's life does not consist in the abundance of possessions." Then, as he usually did, Jesus told a story.

Jesus said that "the land of a rich man produced abundantly." Don't miss the fact that the man in the parable was already rich. This is not a story about some poor migrant farm worker waiting for a green card. This is the story of a guy who already had more than he needed. By the standards of most of the people in most of the rest of the world, he was just like every one of us who, simply because we were "smart enough" to get ourselves born in this country, already consume more than our fair share of the earth's wealth and resources.

Jesus said that this already-rich farmer had a bumper crop. A literal translation of the Greek text would say that his land "produced in super-abundance." It was more than he ever expected, more than he needed, more than he had earned or deserved.

The rich man's bumper crop created a dilemma. Jesus said that the rich man "thought to himself" (verse 17). Don't miss that phrase. He confronted the dilemma of his super-abundance with no reference to God or to anyone else. He doesn't even consult his tax attorney. Even his thought world is confined within the narrow limitations of his own self-interest.

Notice the first-person pronouns in his debate with himself. "He thought to himself, 'What should *I* do, for *I* have no place to store *my* crops?' " Then he answered his own question, "*I* will pull down *my* barns and build larger ones, and there *I* will store all *my* grain and *my* goods. And *I* will say to *my* soul, 'Soul, you have ample goods laid up for many years; relax, eat, drink, be merry' " (emphasis added).

Let's face it: many of the predominant voices in our economic system would call that man a success, a wise investor, a smart businessman. The world would say he was wise, but Jesus had a different perspective. "But God said, 'You fool! Tonight is the night your soul will be required of you' " (Luke 12:20*a*, author's translation). The Greek word translated as "required" is the same word that was used to describe repayment of a debt. "And the things you have prepared, hoarded, stored up in your barns, held for yourself, whose will they be?" (Luke 12:20*b*, paraphrased).

Jesus made the point of the parable crystal clear: "So it is with those who store up treasures for themselves but are not rich toward God" (Luke 12:21). Eugene Peterson paraphrased Jesus' words to say, "That's what happens when you fill your barn with Self and not with God" (*The Message*). The parable reminds me of the story of the day-laborers who watched John D. Rockefeller's funeral procession go by. One asked, "How much did he leave?" The other replied, "All of it."

God called the rich farmer a fool because he was possessed by his possessions. He believed that the abundance of his life was measured by the abundance of things he owned.

The Bible says that greed and envy are foolish because they ultimately consume the consumer in an insatiable desire for more. Enough is never enough. Greed and envy are sinful because they turn our hearts away from the self-giving love of an extravagantly generous God and blind us to the needs of others, so that our entire world becomes defined by what we possess. "Such is the end of all who are greedy for gain; / it takes away the life of its possessors" (Proverbs 1:19).

It's easy for preachers to rail against the evil of greed while secretly envying the rich person's wealth or, at best, hoping that it ends up in the church's coffers. I like to tell the story of the wealthy town scoundrel who asked the preacher, "If I leave all my wealth to the church, will it get me into heaven?" The preacher scratched his head and replied, "Well, it's worth a try!"

But Jesus didn't attack or abuse rich people. In this parable in Luke 12, Jesus never suggests that the rich man is evil. Jesus says that he is foolish. Jesus didn't come to condemn, but to give life. In short, Jesus wants to help rich folks—and all of us—break free from the deadly grip of greed. He wants to liberate us from the soul-shrinking chains of envy. He said he came to give us abundant life; super-abundant life beyond anything we can ask or think. Not abundant in possessions that moth and rust consume, that thieves break in and steal, or that ultimately are passed on to someone else, but life that is abundant with the Spirit of God; life that is like the God who gives it; life that is rich in self-giving love, in compassion, in generosity, and in joy. He offers a few grace-filled steps that will lead us out of the darkness of greed into the new life of resurrection.

Jesus invites us to rejoice in the extravagant creativity of God.

"Consider," Jesus said, "the birds of the air and the flowers of the field" (Matthew 6:26, 28, paraphrased). Look at the extravagant beauty, the health, the provision of nature the way God intended it to function, and remember that the God who creates all of it is the God who loves you as God's own child. Remember that the God who provides for the flowers of the field and the birds of the air is the God who wants to provide for you. Remember that everything you have is on loan to you from an extravagantly creative God.

After he survived a heart attack during the filming of *Apocalypse Now*, actor Martin Sheen returned to his Roman Catholic roots. He said, "I am trying to develop a way of thinking which demands a change in the way I live. . . . I'm still in love with riches and comforts, cars and homes and honors. But I know that either I have to let go of that, or it will all be taken away." Regarding his children, the actor confessed, "It's a painful thing to witness the materialism of my kids, but I know it's only a reflection of what they learned from me. . . . I'm not going to change anyone's life, but I *can* change mine" (*Context*, Claretian Publications, December 15, 1985, page 3).

Jesus invites us to rest in the extravagant goodness of God.

Here is Eugene Peterson's paraphrase of Luke 12:29-31:

> What I'm trying to do here is to get you to relax, not be so preoccupied with *getting* so you can respond to God's *giving*. People who don't know God and the way he works fuss over these things, but you know both God and how he works. Steep yourself in God-reality, God-initiative, God-provisions. You'll find all your everyday human concerns will be met. Don't be afraid of missing out. The Father wants to give you the very kingdom itself. (*The Message*)

This is not, of course, a recipe for laziness. This parable is followed by two of Jesus' parables about the "good and faithful servants." But most of us in our upwardly mobile, high-achieving, work-addicted culture have gotten that message. The word for all of us who are broken by workaholism is to lighten up, to let go a little, to stop grasping and grabbing and start living the way God intends for us to live.

Ann Nelson was thirty years old when she died in the World Trade Center on September 11, 2001. She had left her laptop computer at home when she went to work that day. Afterward, it remained untouched in her parents home in North Dakota because it was simply too painful to face, and because they were not computer savvy.

Eventually, Ann's mother learned how to get into the computer and found a file labeled "Top 100." It contained the goals that Ann had set for her life, including "be a good friend, keep in touch with the people I love and that love me, make a quilt, never be ashamed of who I am, and appreciate money but don't worship it" (*The New York Times*, May 17, 2006, as quoted in *The Christian Century*, June 13, 2006, page 6). I don't know whether Ann was a Christian, but I'd say she had learned to live the way Christ intended.

Jesus invites us to reflect the extravagant generosity of God.

Here is Peterson's paraphrase of Luke 12:33:

> Be generous. Give to the poor. Get yourselves a bank that can't go bankrupt, a bank in heaven far from bankrobbers, safe from embezzlers, a bank you can bank on. It's obvious, isn't it? The

place where your treasure is, is the place you will most want to be, and end up being. (*The Message*, page 178)

One of John Wesley's best known—and perhaps least practiced—sermons is titled "On the Use of Money." Mr. Wesley called money "an excellent gift of God. . . . In the hands of his children . . . a lifter up from the gates of death." His guidance to the early Methodists was defined by three basic rules: "Gain all you can. Save all you can. Give all you can."

We American Methodists have done better on the first two of John Wesley's directives than on the third, but it is the third that makes his instructions Christlike. Anyone can tell us to gain all we can. Anyone can tell us to save all we can. That's exactly what the rich farmer did. But life in the kingdom of God is measured not in how much we gain or how much we save, but in how much we give. It's defined by the way we share our life, our talents, our wealth, and our resources with a world in need. It's the evidence that we have learned that our life is not defined by what we possess.

Wesley practiced what he preached. He determined the amount that he needed to live on and maintained that level of income for the rest of his life, giving the rest of his income to support the early Methodist movement and meet the needs of the poor. Rick Warren, author of the best-selling book *The Purpose-Driven Life,* has followed a similar pattern.

When Warren's book began to break all the records for sales of a religious book, he and his wife had to decide how to live with their newfound wealth. Through prayerful reflection on scripture, they made several fundamental decisions. First, they decided that in spite of all the money that was coming in, they would not change their lifestyle but would continue to live at the same economic level. When I heard him tell his story, he said they were still driving the same car.

Warren's second decision was to stop taking a salary from the Saddleback Church, where he serves as pastor. He added up all that the church had paid him in the twenty-four years he had been its pastor and gave it all back. He said he discovered that it was liberating to be able to serve God for free.

Warren's third step was to set up foundations to initiate what he calls "the P.E.A.C.E. Plan." It is designed to plant churches, equip church leaders, assist the poor, care for the sick, and educate the next generation of Christian leaders. Rick Warren has taken a special interest in the AIDS crisis in Africa and is challenging other church leaders to get on board to make a difference. He found the wisdom that the "rich fool" missed.

I was surprised to receive a check in the mail from a very successful young businessman in Atlanta. He tracked me down through the Internet. I didn't remember him, but he remembered me. Three decades ago, he was a teenager attending our United Methodist youth camp when I was the preacher there. During one of those weeks at summer camp, he made a commitment to Christ that has shaped the rest of his life, and he wanted me to know about it.

He told me that in addition to his regular giving to his local church, he had included the youth camp in his estate plan. As we reminisced about our experiences at the camp, I told him about the way our church has been raising money to send kids from the inner city to camp for more years than anyone can remember. A few days later, a check came in the mail for our camp fund as an expression of gratitude for what God did in his life more than a quarter of a century ago.

That young man had learned the lesson Jesus wants us to learn to heal our broken places of envy and greed. The abundance of life is not defined by the abundance of our possessions, but what we do with our possessions bears witness to the extravagant generosity of God. It's the grace that can lead us out of the dark place of greed or envy, into the life and light of resurrection.

CHAPTER SIX

Sloth: To Care and Not to Care

Teach us to care and not to care
Teach us to sit still.

—T. S. Eliot, "Ash Wednesday"

If lust and greed feel like high-octane, high-risk sins, perhaps it's time to slow things down by turning to the comfortable, lazy sin that is traditionally known as *sloth*. Now, there's a word you don't hear very often outside a zoo, which is precisely the place to begin.

The sloth has the dubious distinction of being the slowest mammal on earth. Sloths spend most of their lives hanging upside down in trees in the rainforests of South and Central America. They rarely venture to the ground and only seldom walk in an upright position. They are solitary and shy and they sleep fifteen to eighteen hours each day. They protect themselves by fading into the lush canopy of the trees, often growing algae on their fur coats so that they simply disappear among the leaves. Most of the time, you don't even know they are there. And let's face it: there may be a lot of us hurried, harried, and hustled workaholics who would say, "Wow! What a life!"

The sloth is the animal kingdom image of what the church fathers had in mind when they identified *sloth* as one of the deadly sins. Saint Thomas Aquinas defined *sloth* as a "sluggishness of the mind which . . . so oppresses man as to draw him away entirely from good deeds." He called it "an oppressive sorrow, which so weighs upon man's mind, that he wants to do nothing."

The Roman Catholic Catechism calls sloth "the desire for ease, even at the expense of doing the known will of God. . . . The slothful person is unwilling to do what God wants because of the effort it takes to do it."

But the sin of sloth goes deeper than just being lazy. It's rooted in the Greek word *acedia*, which literally means "no care." Sloth is the negation of care. The British theologian and dramatist Dorothy L. Sayers put it well when she wrote, "It is the sin that believes in nothing, cares for nothing, seeks to know nothing, interferes with nothing, enjoys nothing, loves nothing, hates nothing, finds purpose in nothing, lives for nothing and remains alive only because there is nothing it would die for" (http://www.geocities.com/ Heartland/2964/homily-1lent-a.html).

If the words of ancient church fathers and British theologians require just a little more mental energy than you care to expend, it's hard to improve on the country song by Travis Tritt that says, "Here's a quarter, call someone who cares." Sloth is the apathy that results from not caring. It's a dark, lonely, loveless place where we shrivel up and ultimately die in the lonely boredom of self-interest. It's the broken place where passion and care are reduced to indolence and the carelessness that results from caring less.

I'm convinced that healing in the broken place of sloth does not mean becoming a workaholic, which is an addiction I inherited from my father and for which I have been in recovery for the better part of my adult life. It seems to me that T. S. Eliot captured the better solution when he wrote

Suffer us not to mock ourselves with falsehood
Teach us to care and not to care
Teach us to sit still
Even among these rocks,
Our peace in His will.
(*Modern American Poetry*, Harcourt, Brace & World, 1962,
page 402)

Jesus painted an unforgettable picture of what it means "to care and not to care" in the story of a man we call "the good Samaritan," recorded in Luke 10:30-37. It begins with a man who is beaten, robbed, and left to die along the road. Then Jesus describes the contrasting responses of the people who found the man there.

Jesus described the priest and the Levite, who saw the man in the road but just walked on by. For all we know, they weren't lazy. I'll bet they were hard-working religious leaders who either had so much on their minds that they didn't even see the man, or were so busy hustling off to their work that they didn't have time to stop. All we know for sure is that they didn't cross over to the other side of the road to see what could be done to help the beaten, bruised, nearly lifeless man who had fallen among thieves.

The Samaritan, on the other hand, "was moved with pity" (verse 33). He saw the man in the ditch and he cared. For the Samaritan, caring meant "relinquishing the sin of indifference" (Karl Menninger, *Whatever Became of Sin?* Hawthorne Books, 1973, page 189). Notice the way Jesus piled up the active verbs to describe what it meant for this man to care for the man by the side of the road. Jesus said that he *saw* him, *went* to him, *bandaged* his wounds, *poured* oil and wine on them, *put* him on his own animal, *brought* him to an inn, *took* out two denarii, *gave* them to the innkeeper, and *said*, "Take care of him; and when I come back, I will repay you whatever more you spend" (verse 35).

There's nothing lazy there! Not a passive verb in the story. The Samaritan did a lot of active caring. And there's no ambiguity in the punch line when Jesus said, "Go and do likewise." Followers of Jesus are people who care and who put that caring into action. In the kingdom of God, caring begins as something we feel, but it is expressed in something we do. It is an active response to an observed need. The one thing a follower of Christ cannot say is, "I just don't care."

This kind of active caring is imbedded in the genetic code of the Methodist tradition. Early in his ministry, John Wesley prayed, "Deliver me, O God, from a slothful mind, from all lukewarmness, and all dejection of sprit. I know these cannot but deaden my love to you; mercifully free my heart from them, and give me a lively, zealous, active, and cheerful spirit, that I may vigorously perform whatever you command, thankfully suffer whatever you choose for me, and be ardent to obey in all things your holy love" (*John and Charles Wesley: Selected Writings and Hymns*, page 80).

Wesley's powerful adjectives and adverbs—*lively, zealous, active, cheerful, vigorously perform, thankfully suffer*—capture the energy that sent the early Methodists out into the streets of London to visit the prisons, feed the hungry, and serve the poor. They believed that the only kind of faith that makes a difference is faith that results in active engagement with the needs of the world.

Because it's in our DNA, Methodists have generally been pretty good at expressing care by doing things. If you need someone to get things organized, to make things happen, and to get things done, just call on the Methodists! One well-known history of

American Methodism catches the spirit of it with the subtitle *Organizing to Beat the Devil*.

Methodists have tended to be activist Christians. The dark side of all that activity is that we can develop a raging case of "compassion fatigue." I like to quote the bit of doggerel that says

> Mary had a little lamb
> She also had a sheep
> She joined The United Methodist Church
> And died for lack of sleep.

It can happen, you know. There are so many people by the side of the road, so many needs to be met, so many challenges to fulfill, so many good things to be done, and sometimes, so few people to actually do them that we can simply wear ourselves out with well-doing. (See 2 Thessalonians 3:13.) It happens in relationships. It happens in marriages. It happens in families. We can be so busy, going in so many directions, doing so many good things that we lose ourselves and lose any sense of why we are doing what we do.

Perhaps that's why Luke follows the parable of the good Samaritan with the contrasting story of Mary and Martha (Luke 10:38-42). I have permission to tell you that my wife doesn't like this story very much. My wife's name is Martha, so she is a little sensitive about the bad rap that the biblical Martha often gets because of her actions. Her name is not the only thing my wife has in common with Martha; you should see the way she works in the kitchen when company is coming! And when she starts cleaning house, you'd better just get out of the way. A dust bunny has less chance of survival in our house than a rabbit during hunting season.

My wife knows exactly how Martha felt when she said, "Lord, don't you care? Don't you care that I'm doing all the work around here? Don't you care that Mary is just hanging around your feet like a sloth on a tree limb? How about giving Mary a little of your 'Go and do likewise' speech? How about a little active caring on Mary's part?" (Martha didn't quite say it that way, but that's the way my wife would understand it!)

I can understand both the Martha in the parable and the Martha in my life. In fact, I'm a lot like them. A quick look at my Myers-Briggs personality inventory (for those who care about these things, I'm an ENFJ) confirms that I am something of a hyperactive extrovert who likes to make things happen. Combine my basic personality type with my childhood in the home of a workaholic father, and you have a guy who tends toward finding self-worth in what he accomplishes; a boy who hoped to receive approval from his father on the basis of what he could do or accomplish. I know how it feels to be just a little skeptical about people who seem just a little too passive, quiet, and still to get anything done.

To tell the truth, we "Type A" high-achievers would probably be a lot happier with Jesus if he hadn't responded the way he did. It's a little like the teetotaling temperance woman who was asked how she felt about the fact that Jesus turned water into wine. She replied sternly, "Yes, I know he did, and I'd think better of him if he hadn't." That may be how we feel about the way Jesus responded to Martha. "Martha, Martha. You are worried, distracted, troubled, pulled in every direction by too many things. You're missing the one thing that is really necessary to hold it all together. Mary has latched onto the one thing that won't be taken away from her" (Luke 10:41-42, paraphrased). You can hear in Jesus' words his invitation to Martha to come, sit down, cool her heels, and get in touch with the stuff that really matters.

Some things never change. In the fourth century, Athanasius said that we are like mad charioteers who run with more speed than direction, racing off in all directions but losing sight of the finish line. The truth about some of us is that precisely because we care, because there are so many good things to do, because we are trying to be faithful disciples of Jesus Christ, we can end up running all over the place, without clear priorities or direction, doing so many good things that we lose ourselves in the process.

Norman Shawchuck expressed our need for deep centering in the presence of God when he prayed

> Reach down inside me now, O God, and change the gears that race and roar. In place of turmoil give me peace; in place of frenzy give me patience. Then shall I be more like Jesus, who taught us to make room for you in our hectic days. . . . Then I shall find peace. Then I will be at peace with my self and with you. (*A Guide to Prayer for All Who Seek God*, Upper Room Books, 2003, page 342)

Luke hangs these apparently contradictory portraits in the front room of our imaginations, and inquiring minds want to know: so, which is it? Which portrait captures the way of life in Christ? Is it the good Samaritan, actively caring for the man he picked up along the side of the road? Is it Martha, caring about all the work that needed doing in the kitchen? Is it Mary, caring enough about the words of Jesus to sit at his feet and soak them in? And the answer is, Yes! Luke doesn't even try to reconcile these contrasting portraits. He just hangs them out there and invites us to discover the grace of God in the tension between them.

Eddie Fox is a good-Samaritan, activist type of Christian. He is the director of World Evangelism for the World Methodist Council. Eddie is a high-octane disciple who travels all over the world sharing the gospel of Jesus Christ. Every now and then people will ask Eddie, which is more important in the Christian life: personal piety or social action? Is it the life of meditation and prayer or the life of active engagement with human need? What's the first priority— healing our broken souls or healing the brokenness of the world around us? Eddie's answer is that it's just like breathing. We inhale and exhale; we breathe in and we breathe out. The answer to which is most important depends on which one you did last.

When biographer John Allen tried to sum up the factors that made Desmond Tutu one of the most influential leaders for social change in the twentieth century, he wrote, "The foundations of Tutu's stature and his moral authority are to be found in his spirituality and faith" (*Rabble-Rouser for Peace,* Free Press, 2006, page 394). According to Allen, Tutu lives with the constant tension between his need and desire for a life of solitude and prayer on one hand, and his compassion for those who suffer and his anger at injustice on the other. "Tutu the ebullient extrovert and Tutu the meditative priest who needed six or seven hours a day in silence were two sides of the same coin. One could not exist without the other: in particular, his extraordinary capacity to communicate with warmth, compassion, and humor depended on the regeneration of personal resources, which in turn depended on the iron self-discipline of his prayers" (*Rabble-Rouser for Peace,* page 275).

And so we return to T. S. Eliot's prayer: "Teach us to care and not to care." Sometimes the broken place in our lives is our lack of care for the needs of a broken world. In those times, we need to walk down the road that leads to Jericho, where we meet the good Samaritan and hear Jesus' command, "Go and do likewise." Sometimes the broken place is deep in our own soul as a result of our lack of prayer, worship, and reflection on scripture. In those times we need to hear Jesus say, much as he did to Martha, "You're distracted by so many things. Sit down with me for a while and I'll help you sort out the things that really matter."

There is a time to care and a time not to care; a time for activity and a time for silence; a time to get off our duff and get to work, and a time to get down on our knees and pray. The sin is in saying we just don't care. The grace comes in knowing the difference.

CHAPTER SEVEN

Gluttony: Super-sized Sin

I find myself very disturbed lately by the fact that restaurants give you more than any sane person would want to eat. . . . I'm very aware, almost for the first time in my life, of consumerism, being a dupe of consumerism.

—*John Updike,* TIME Magazine *(June 5, 2006)*

It's a rare and lucky day for a preacher when an academic research paper, a documentary movie, and a bishop's sermon all converge on the same subject. It almost sounds like the opening line of a bad joke: "A professor, a producer, and a bishop all walk into a bar . . ." But there they were in my imagination, barging into my study and gathering around my computer just in time to find their way into this chapter on gluttony.

The professor is Ken Ferraro, a sociologist at Purdue University, who has studied connections between religion and body weight since the early 1990s. "America is becoming known as a nation of gluttony and obesity," he said, "and churches are a feeding ground for this problem."

After studying 2,500 people over eight years, he found that some religious practices such as prayer, meditation, and the social interaction provided by a religious community are good for people's health. Some of his studies found that people who read the Bible more often have lower blood pressure, and people who are more religious are less likely to be depressed. But he also found that although "most religions also encourage restraint from participating in injurious behaviors, such as heavy drinking and smoking . . . overeating is not considered a great sin—it has become the accepted vice." He challenged religious leaders to model physical health as a necessary part of spiritual discipline and well-being (http://www.purdue.edu/UNS/html4ever/2006/060824.Ferraro .obesity.html).

The movie producer is Morgan Spurlock, whose controversial film *Super Size Me*, was nominated for an Academy Award for best documentary film. Spurlock ate a steady diet at McDonald's for thirty days. The film documented in disgusting detail the deterioration of his physical and emotional health to make the point that the food we Americans are eating really is killing us.

The bishop is Sally Dyck, who presides over the Minnesota Annual Conference of The United Methodist Church. On Ash Wednesday one year, she challenged the Minnesota clergy to think of Lent as forty days in a "spiritual spa," during which they should indulge themselves by adopting healthier eating habits. She called on them to join her in eating five to nine "clean" fruits and vegetables a day, exercising at least thirty minutes a day, and praying and reading the Bible for thirty minutes each day. By "clean" she specifically meant fruits and vegetables devoid of the "Minnesota favorites" of butter, sour cream, mayonnaise, or cream that often drown fruit and vegetables in that area. I guess those foods are to Minnesota what fried chicken is in the South! To make things interesting, the bishop promised to donate two dollars to fight world hunger for every pound her clergy lost before Easter. One pastor warned her, "You could lose a lot of money there, Bishop" (www.umc.org/interior.asp?mid=6882).

Gluttony, defined as "excessive indulgence in food and drink," is the place where the world—particularly our contemporary American culture—breaks many of us. In writing about it, I want to carefully separate the sin of gluttony from the medical conditions of anorexia and bulimia, both of which call for special medical care. Sin, including this one, involves some element of choice on the part of the sinner.

One of the Latin words that the early church fathers used to describe gluttony comes from the same root word as *voracious*. We can, of course, be gluttonous about almost anything—wealth, power, pleasure, sex, possessions. We Americans are voracious in our consumption of our natural resources. Some of us struggle with "gadget gluttony," the insatiable desire to have every new piece of technology that comes off the line, and preferably have it before anyone else. But in the long tradition of the church, gluttony has generally focused on what medieval theologian Thomas Aquinas called "an inordinate desire for food and drink going beyond the limits of reason." And the evidence is that Aquinas's definition is still accurate for us today.

The National Institutes of Health say that at least one third of the American population is overweight to a degree that is unhealthy. The standard width of store aisles has expanded from five feet to seven-and-a-half feet, not only because of customer size but also because the shopping carts are getting bigger, reflecting our voracious appetite for more and more stuff. On the national average, our families are getting smaller while our houses are getting larger, because we need more space for all of our stuff. We are voracious consumers. It even follows us in death. The standard width for caskets has long been twenty-four inches, but now, the Goliath Casket Company is making expanded double-wides, up to fifty-two inches. The casket itself weighs over 200 pounds, which is enough to send any prospective pallbearer straight to the gym.

It's easy enough to rail against the gluttonous consumption of our culture, but there's not much evidence that the railing is making much of a difference. On top of that, there is no grace in negative attacks. So, what will it mean for us to find God's grace in the dark places of our voracious appetites? How does the grace of God bring healing to the broken place of gluttony?

Fortunately for us, the Christians in Corinth were just about as gluttonous as we are, providing a setting in which to hear some radical, indeed counter-cultural words from the apostle Paul.

First, the apostle offers a radical word about our bodies.

The culture in which the Corinthian Christians lived assumed a near-total separation between the physical world, which was assumed to be evil, and the spiritual world, which was assumed to be good. The result was that there was little connection between religious experience and bodily practice. It didn't matter what you did with your body, just so long as your spirit was in good shape. That assumption seeped into Christianity in the heresy of Gnosticism, which is still alive and well among us today. It's the assumption that these physical bodies don't really matter; they are just dusty shells to house an eternal spirit that will someday escape and go somewhere else.

But along came the Christian message of the Incarnation—the earthshaking story of the One who came to be "God with us." The early Christians proclaimed that Jesus was really God and really one of us. The Gospel of John declared, "The Word became flesh and lived among us" (John 1:14). As a result, Paul took a radically different view of our bodies. It must have surprised the folks in Corinth to hear him say, "The body is meant . . . for the Lord, and the Lord for the body. And God raised the Lord and will also raise us [our bodies] by his power. Do you not know that your bodies are members of Christ?" (1 Corinthians 6:13-15).

That was shocking stuff! Paul did not say that we have an eternal spirit that is somehow connected with Christ and will go on living after our bodies die. He declared that our physical bodies are actually members of the body of Christ. Paul went on to say, "Your body is a temple of the Holy Spirit within you, which you have from God . . . you are not your own" (1 Corinthians 6:19). These bodies are not our privately held playthings to do with as we choose, because, as Paul continues in verse 20, "You were bought with a price; therefore glorify God in your body."

If the Corinthians didn't take their bodies seriously enough, there is a good possibility that we sometimes take our bodies too seriously, with near cultic worship of the outward appearance of what the culture defines as the perfect body. Waiting at the newsstand in the airport, I did some research in the men's section of the magazines. I'm sure the same principle would be true in the women's section. There appeared to be two kinds of magazine covers. One cover has women who really don't look like most of the women I know. The others have men whose bodies are so perfectly chiseled that they evidently spend all their time in the gym. But walking down the concourse, looking at the real people around me, it became immediately apparent that there are a lot more average, ordinary, imperfect bodies out there than there are the kind of bodies that appear on the magazine covers.

To tell you the truth, I hope that Jesus didn't have one of those perfect, magazine-cover bodies. I hope he had a very ordinary body like yours or mine, because that's just how radical the Incarnation is meant to be. The Word became flesh—real flesh, ordinary flesh, imperfect flesh like every one of us.

Paul also has a radical word about discipline and freedom.

In 1 Corinthians 6:12, Paul enters into debate with the Corinthians. Some folks there evidently were saying, "All things are lawful for me." The New English Bible gets the translation a little more clearly, when it has the Corinthians say, "I am free to do anything." Paul replies, "Yes, you're free to do anything, but not all things are beneficial." Again, they say, "All things are lawful"; but Paul says, "Ah, yes, but I will not be dominated by anything" (1 Corinthians 6:12, paraphrased). J. B. Phillips makes the point by translating Paul's words this way: "As a Christian I *may* do anything, but that does not mean that everything is good for me. I may do everything, but I must not be a slave of anything" (*The New Testament in Modern English*, rev. ed., Macmillan, 1958).

Paul sets up two fences of discipline around our freedom. First, is the way I treat my body beneficial? And second, is my behavior dominating or taking control of me? Those are good questions to ask about any of our appetites. Is it beneficial for my physical, emotional, spiritual, and relational health and well-being? Is it beneficial to myself and to others? And is it taking control of me? Am I being dominated by my desire for it?

The bishop in Minnesota was calling for a similar attitude when she invited her pastors into a Lenten "spiritual spa" where they could develop healthy physical disciplines. It's what I read in an e-mail message from a friend whom I see running along Tampa's Bayshore Boulevard in the morning:

> I hope when you see me in the morning on the Bayshore that you will realize that you are witnessing a religious experience. I am so thankful for this miraculous machine that God has created. I cannot let a day pass without coming to this altar. I don't know how you will touch on this, but in my mind there is no more important "sin" than to forsake one's responsibility to care for our personal "temple."

The Christian faith calls us to a balance of freedom and discipline that will enable us to move out of the bondage of our voracious appetites and into a life of wholeness and well-being, a life that glorifies God with our bodies.

When I was working on this chapter, I came across "The No S Diet." It's described as "a few simple, mnemonic tricks for giving your willpower the upper hand." There are three rules and one exception:

No Snacks
No Sweets
No Seconds
Except (sometimes) on days that start with "s".
(www.nosdiet.com/?ad)

The balance of discipline and freedom doesn't get much simpler than that!

Paul offers a radical word about our spiritual hunger for wholeness.

Cornelius Plantinga, Jr., writes about "spiritual hygiene" as the wholeness of life the way God intended it.

> Self-indulgence tends to suppress gratitude; self-discipline tends to generate it. That is why gluttony is a deadly sin: oddly, it is an appetite suppressant. The reason is that a person's appetites are linked: full stomachs and jaded palates take the edge from our hunger and thirst for justice. They spoil the appetite for God. (*Not the Way It's Supposed to Be*, Eerdmans, 1995, page 35)

Frederick Buechner said that a glutton is a person "who raids the ice box to find a cure for spiritual malnutrition" (*Wishful Thinking*, Harper & Row, 1973, page 31). The struggle with gluttony is often the outward and visible sign of an inward and spiritual hunger for acceptance, love, or self-worth. Sometimes it is the result of a broken place in our past that separates us from others and isolates us from healthy relationships. The deepest hunger in our lives is always the hunger and thirst for God. That hunger will not be quenched by all of the stuff we consume.

Lest this chapter appear to be a call to some sort of life-draining diet of self-denial, let's close with the reminder that when the biblical writers attempted to paint a picture of the wholeness of human life in relationship with God, they often described a feast. The Old Testament prophet Isaiah painted the picture of a banquet that would make any gourmet drool.

On this mountain the LORD of hosts will make for all peoples
    a feast of rich food, a feast of well-aged wines,
    of rich food filled with marrow, of well-aged wines strained clear.
And he will destroy on this mountain
    the shroud that is cast over all peoples,
    the sheet that is spread over all nations;
    he will swallow up death forever.
Then the Lord GOD will wipe away the tears from all faces,
    and the disgrace of his people he will take away from all the earth,
    for the LORD has spoken. (Isaiah 25:6-8)

Jesus described the kingdom of God as "a king who gave a wedding banquet for his son," to which everyone was invited (Matthew 22:2-14). When the apostle John attempted to describe the fulfillment of the reign of Christ at the end of time, he painted the picture of "the marriage supper of the Lamb" (Revelation 19:9). And when Jesus wanted to give us a way to remember him, he gathered his disciples around a dinner table, broke the bread, blessed the wine, and said that they represented his body and blood, given for them.

The writer of the eighty-first psalm described the way God satisfies the deepest hungers of our souls when he heard God say, "I would feed you with the finest of the wheat, / and with honey from the rock I would satisfy you" (Psalm 81:16).

The psalmist's words are often sung around the communion table in the contemporary hymn that says, "You satisfy the hungry heart with gift of finest wheat" (Omer Westendorf, "The Gift of Finest Wheat," *The United Methodist Hymnal*, no. 629).

Perhaps the healing of gluttony comes not in "super-sizing" our meals, but in a super-sized awareness of the goodness and grace of God!

CHAPTER EIGHT

Anger: The Froggy Gremlin in All of Us

I have always felt that a raised voice was a mistake.

—*Kim Stafford*, Early Morning: Remembering My Father, William Stafford

You need to be of a certain age to appreciate the title of this chapter. Baby Boomers heading into retirement will quickly remember Froggy the Gremlin from the 1950s Saturday morning television show *Andy's Gang*.

Scratchy-voiced Andy Devine, who also showed up in a lot of TV westerns, hosted the show with a bleacher full of children on the set. It featured Andy's animal friends, Midnight the Cat and Squeaky the Mouse, along with the weekly installment of the story of "Gunga, the East India Boy." But the biggest response from the kids came every week when Andy would walk over to his grandfather clock and call out, "Plunk your magic twanger, Froggy!" I can't remember ever wondering exactly what a "twanger" was, or what it might mean to plunk it! There would be a puff of smoke, and Froggy the Gremlin would pop out, saying, "Hiya, kids! Hiya! Hiya!"

Froggy was a feisty little guy who was constantly pulling nasty tricks on Andy. There was a mean streak in Froggy, the same sort of mean streak that shows up in most of us sometimes. In fact, I'm pretty sure that there is a Froggy the Gremlin hiding inside each of us, ready to pop out and cause trouble with little more than a plunk of our magic twanger—whatever that is!

Cornelius Plantinga, Jr., defines *anger* as "passionate against-ness." He says that anger always has "a posture of antagonism." It always gets turned against someone or something (*Not the Way It's Supposed to Be,* Eerdmans, 1995, page 165). Maxie Dunnam defines two kinds of anger: the blazing kind and the brooding kind. There's anger that explodes like a powder keg, and anger that sim-mers like a Crock Pot (*The Workbook on the Seven Deadly Sins,* Upper Room Books, 1995, page 83).

However we experience it, anger is the gremlin inside us. It is clearly the most complex of all of our emotions. As a starting point, it's hard to beat the simplicity of the apostle Paul's words in Ephesians 4:26: "Be angry but do not sin."

Those words were not original with Paul. The writer of the fourth psalm said, "Be angry, and do not sin; ponder in your own hearts on your beds" (Psalm 4:4 English Standard Translation). The first part of the command indicates that there are times when we need to "be angry." The Bible never says that there is anything inherently sinful about the emotion of anger. It is, in fact, a healthy, normal, and, in some ways, necessary emotion.

In his book *Embodying Forgiveness,* L. Gregory Jones writes that anger can be "a work of love" when it expresses "a moral protest" against the power of evil, suffering, death, and sin (Eerdmans, 1995, page 246). I've spent enough hours with people who face raging injustice, irrational suffering, and irreparable grief to know that anger can be the voice of God within us that shouts, "This isn't right! It isn't fair! This is not the way it's supposed to be!"

And yet, anger is a difficult emotion for many Christian people to accept. We will, albeit reluctantly, confess that we are lusty, greedy, envious, slothful, gluttonous people. But most of us have a hard time acknowledging our anger. We tend to mask it, hide it, or give it other names—almost anything to avoid saying, "I'm angry." In more than a dozen years of interviewing candidates for ordained ministry, I discovered that they had more difficulty with anger than any other emotion. And the more the interviewer would attempt to penetrate the denial, the stronger the denial would become.

But there are times when, like Jesus and the Old Testament prophets before him, we should be angry. There are times when, like the lead character in the 1976 movie *Network*, we shout, "I'm as mad as hell, and I'm not going to take this anymore!" (http://www.americanrhetoric.com/MovieSpeeches/moviespeech network2.html).

Jesus was angry, the Gospel says, when the scribes and Pharisees were more interested in keeping the law than in healing a withered hand (see Mark 3:1-6); when they were more intent on protecting their self-interest and national security than in being the agents of God's salvation (see John 11:47-52); when they cleaned up the outside of their lives but were rotten at the core (see Matthew 23:12-39).

As I read these passages, it strikes me that perhaps the reason religious folks have such a hard time acknowledging anger is because they realize that self-righteous religious folks were the ones who ticked Jesus off the most.

Jesus was angry when he watched the money changers use the Temple tax system to take advantage of the poor while turning a hefty profit for the rich (see Matthew 21:12-13). Jesus expressed anger toward anyone who hurt, abused, or neglected a child (see Matthew 18:6). Jesus was deeply moved—the New Living Translation says "moved with indignation"—when he faced the awful reality of death at the tomb of his friend Lazarus (see John 11:33). Jesus wept in frustrated sorrow when he looked out over the city of Jerusalem and said, "If only you knew the things that make for peace" (Luke 19:42, paraphrased).

These outbursts of divine anger are, to be sure, exceptional moments in the gospel. They are not the dominant characteristic of Jesus' life, but they demonstrate that the more deeply we are drawn into Jesus' vision of the kingdom of God, the more deeply we feel moral outrage at everything that blocks the coming of that kingdom on earth as it is already fulfilled in heaven. The more deeply we experience the infinite compassion of God for the poor, the marginalized, the oppressed, the lost, the more deeply we feel divine indignation over everything that contradicts the life-giving, saving purpose of God. The closer we get to the heart of God, the more deeply we know the divine frustration with the almost impenetrable hardness of heart that breaks the heart of God.

Paul said, "Be angry . . ." There is a time for healthy, appropriate anger. But as soon as we've said that, we need to acknowledge that anger is as tricky as Froggy the Gremlin. It's the second part of that biblical command that balances the first: "Be angry, but do not sin." The question is not whether we feel anger, but what we are angry about and the ends toward which our anger is directed. Anger is not sinful in itself, but it becomes sinful and downright deadly depending on what we do with it.

In Ephesians 4:26-27, Paul offers practical advice on dealing with anger: "Do not let the sun go down on your anger, and do not make room for the devil." The New Living Translation paraphrases Psalm 4:4 to say, "Don't sin by letting anger gain control over you." Don't allow your anger to create a room in your soul where the devil can take up residence and ultimately take control of your life. Watch out for the way the broken place of anger can become a dank, dismal basement in which our souls grow sour, our spirits shrink, and our hearts become moldy and cold.

Reflecting on Paul's guidance to the Ephesians, L. Gregory Jones concludes, "Anger can be legitimate if it is in the service of God's inbreaking Kingdom. . . . But anger can also lead to sin, particularly if it is allowed to ossify into hatred and desires for revenge" (*Embodying Forgiveness*, page 247).

It's interesting to see the contrast between the things that caused anger for Jesus and the things that caused the religious leaders and political rulers of the day to be angry enough to nail him to the cross. Jesus' anger was rooted in God's mercy and love and was directed against anything that contradicted the life-giving, loving, saving purpose of God. But the anger of those who turned against Jesus was anger because his words and way threatened their self-interest, security, pride, power, and control. Jesus' anger was a compassionate response to the suffering of others; their anger was their response to anything that threatened their self-interest.

There's nothing sinful about the emotion of anger, particularly when it is anger over the things that break the heart of God. But anger becomes sinful when we allow it to take control of us; when we act out our anger in ways that are not consistent with the way of Christ; when it hardens into resentment, revenge, or hostility.

Anger becomes deadly when instead of leading us into deeper paths of obedience, service, and compassion, it results in rage, manipulation, violence, and death; when divine indignation at the evil actions of others is used to justify our doing the same thing; when the way we deal with our anger leads us to become the mirror image of the evils we oppose.

"Don't let the sun go down on your anger" means not allowing our anger to take control of us. Don't make room for the devil to take up residence in your soul. In his letter to Rome, Paul said, "Do not be overcome by evil, but overcome evil with good" (Romans 12:21).

I learned this lesson from a couple in the first church I served. She was consistently one of the grouchiest, unhappiest, most miserable people I've ever met. When she walked into the room, the sunlight seemed to be driven out. You had the feeling that if she smiled, something might break. He had the appearance of a kicked dog that could either snap back or slink away if you came too near.

One Sunday afternoon she called and told me that they needed to see me right away. Looking back, my guess is that every pastor who served that church got the same call, but I didn't realize it then. I headed over to their house without a clue as to what the crisis might be. The house was just as joyless as they were. The anger in the room was as dark and thick as the drapes that covered the windows. The weary sadness of the home was consistent with the joyless expression on their faces.

I had barely gotten in the door when she began to pour out her anger at the way her husband had betrayed her by having an affair with her best friend. Every painful detail hung in the air as if it had happened the night before. I'll confess that I was a little amazed at this because both of them had been receiving their Social Security checks longer than I had been in the ministry. After she had poured out the venom of her anger, I turned to him. He acknowledged what had happened and said that he had asked her to forgive him, but she didn't seem to be able to do it. Then something prompted me to ask, "When did this happen?" She snarled back, "Thirty-five years ago!"

That's when I understood why Paul told us not to let the sun go down on our anger and not to allow the devil to take up that kind of residence in your life. That's when I learned how the darkness of unresolved anger can block the light of life and love in our souls.

One of my problems with many of the loudest voices from the "Religious Right" is not so much what they say, but how they say it. Their venomous anger sounds a lot more like the self-righteous anger of the Pharisees than the brokenhearted anger of Jesus.

So, how do we deal with the deadly gremlin of anger? How do we experience God's grace in the broken place of anger in our lives? From the many words that the Bible has to say about this, let me offer two words of practical guidance for us.

First, slow down. The writer of the epistle of James advises any of us who are prone to anger, "You must understand this, my beloved: let everyone be quick to listen, slow to speak, slow to anger, for your anger does not produce God's righteousness" (James 1:19-20).

I confess that far too often, I get that backwards. Far too often, I am slow to listen, but quick to speak and quick to anger because I have the mistaken impression that somehow my anger can result in the righteousness of God. But James turns it the other way around. He challenges us to be quick to listen, slow to speak, and slow to become angry, because our human anger can never produce the goodness and righteousness of God.

Be quick to listen to your own anger. Where is it coming from? What is it about? Is it born out of the infinite mercy and compassion of God? Or is it born out of human envy, pride, greed, selfishness, the need for control? Is it in proportion to the immediate cause? Or is it misdirected anger coming from somewhere else?

Be quick to listen to the anger of others. Listen to the persons who are angry with you. What are they really saying? What is the root of their anger? What can we learn from it?

Slow down. Be quick to listen, but slow to speak and slow to act on your anger, because your anger can never result in the goodness or righteousness of God.

Second, look up to the cross. Paul advises us, "Put away from you all bitterness and wrath and anger and wrangling and slander, together with all malice, and be kind to one another, tenderhearted, forgiving one another, as God in Christ has forgiven you" (Ephesians 4:31-32). The grace of God that meets us in our anger is the amazing grace of the God who forgives our trespasses as we forgive those who trespass against us, and who demonstrates that forgiveness at the cross.

The most amazing example of the power of both evil and forgiveness in recent history has to be the work of the Truth and Reconciliation Commission in dealing with the aftermath of Apartheid in South Africa. Desmond Tutu tells the story in his book *No Future Without Forgiveness*. Listen to what he says they learned through that process.

Forgiving and being reconciled are not about pretending that things are other than they are. It is not patting one another on the back and turning a blind eye to the wrong. True reconciliation exposes the awfulness, the abuse, the pain, the degradation, the truth. It could even sometimes make things worse. It is a risky undertaking but in the end it is worthwhile, because in the end dealing with the real situation helps bring real healing. . . .

In forgiving, people are not asked to forget. On the contrary, it is important to remember, so that we should not let such atrocities happen again. Forgiveness does not mean condoning what has been done. It means taking what happened seriously and not minimizing it; drawing out the string in the memory that threatens to poison our entire existence. . . .

Forgiving means abandoning your right to pay back the perpetrator in his own coin, but it is a loss that liberates the victim. (*No Future Without Forgiveness*, Image, 2000, pages 271-72)

The grace of God that meets us in the broken place of our anger is nothing less than the forgiving grace that meets us at the cross. There is no future without it.

CHAPTER NINE
Pride: Let Your High Horse Die

When I can be strong but humble in the face of a difficult task, I can begin without fear. Humility is power. To be common but right, to be ordinary but clear is to be difficult to defeat. . . . The aggressor's force becomes an advantage to the pliant but resilient resistor.

—*Kim Stafford,* Early Morning: Remembering My Father, William Stafford

Have you ever ridden on a donkey? When I was a teenager we had some friends who lived on a farm and raised burros, which is another name for a small donkey. A lanky teenager or a full-grown adult would hang all over the thing. The burros were temperamental too, particularly when they sensed that the person on their back was a city person who didn't have a clue as to what they were doing when they visited a farm. More than once, I went out over the head of the burro when he locked his knees, bent his neck, and decided to put his rider on the ground. You might be able to feel important on the back of a horse, but it's easy to feel downright stupid on a donkey.

Jesus must have looked downright silly that day, riding into Jerusalem on a donkey—a foal, the text says, not even a full-grown donkey, just a little donkey. Jesus' legs must have been dangling down so that his toes scraped the road, and his robe must have been dragging in the dust. To tell the truth, he must have looked more like a clown than a king.

Matthew makes the picture even more absurd by making it sound as if Jesus rode two donkeys at the same time. He was quoting Zechariah, who had used poetic Hebrew parallelism to underscore the meekness of a king who would ride, not on a war horse, but on a donkey—not even a full-sized donkey, but the foal of a donkey. Matthew, perhaps just a little too literal in his desire to connect Jesus with the Old Testament prophecy, ends up with two donkeys in Matthew 21:7: "They brought the donkey and the colt, and put their cloaks on them, and he sat on them." It's hard enough to keep your dignity on one donkey; I'd hate to try it on two!

So, there Jesus was on the back of a floppy-eared donkey, loping down the Mount of Olives and into Jerusalem. He must have looked like a Palestinian version of the Beverly Hillbillies, riding their rickety old truck into Los Angeles. To anyone with even a smidgen of pride, position, power, or prestige, it had to be downright laughable—a Monty Python sort of satire; an absurd parody of what the world calls real power.

If you've never pictured the Palm Sunday parade as a sort of visual joke, this is a good time to do it because in this chapter we're thinking together about the broken place in our lives called *pride*.

When the sixth-century pope known as Gregory the Great (which would be a pride-filled name if he had given it to himself!) codified his list of the seven deadly sins, he put pride first because he said it is the cancerous root from which all the other sins grow. It was his vivid description of the way an unhealthy sense of pride is the primary symptom of the brokenness in our lives.

In an earlier chapter, we looked at three biblical principles about sin. We said that sin disrupts, destroys, or damages relationships. We said that sin distorts something good. C. S. Lewis called it "spoiled goodness." And we said that sin is deadly. The consequence of sin is always some kind of death. All three principles apply to what the Bible says about sinful, arrogant, self-indulgent pride.

Sinful pride is "spoiled goodness." It is a destructive distortion of a healthy sense of self-respect. The apostle Paul told the Roman Christians "not to think of yourself more highly than you ought to think, but to think with sober judgment, each according to the measure of faith that God has assigned" (Romans 12:3). J. B. Phillips paraphrased that verse to read, "Don't cherish exaggerated ideas of yourself or your importance, but try to have a sane estimate of your capabilities by the light of the faith that God has given to you all" (*The New Testament in Modern English*, Macmillan, 1958).

Simply put, healthy pride becomes sinful when we start taking ourselves too seriously; when, instead of having a "sane estimate" of our human capabilities, we become insanely addicted to our own importance. C. S. Lewis said that the root of all sin is "being too big for your boots, forgetting your place, thinking that you are God" (*The Quotable Lewis*, Tyndale House, 1989, page 214).

G. K. Chesterton, with his acerbic British wit, captured the inherent foolishness of sinful pride when he described it as "the downward drag of all things into an easy solemnity. One 'settles down' into a sort of selfish seriousness; but one has to rise to a gay self-forgetfulness." Chesterton said that seriousness is not a virtue, but is a tendency of "taking one's self gravely. . . . It is easy to be heavy: hard to be light. Satan fell by force of gravity. . . . Angels can fly because they take themselves so lightly" (*Orthodoxy*, Doubleday, 1959, pages 120-21).

In the same vein, Leonard Sweet said that "since the devil never laughs, a sense of humor is the best weapon in the fight against evil" (*Faithquakes,* Abingdon Press, 1994, page 111). We get into trouble when we start taking ourselves too seriously and lose an appropriate sense of lightness about our human condition. A healthy sense of humor, even a propensity for parody, can offer a healing antidote for a sin-diseased sense of pride.

The writer of the Second Psalm described the arrogance of the kings and rulers of the earth who, in their self-importance and power, set themselves up against the purpose of God. But then the psalmist must have looked up at the cloud, and a smile must have spread across his face when he wrote

> He who sits in the heavens laughs;
> the LORD has them in derision.
> (Psalm 2:4)

All of which invites us to picture Jesus' donkey ride into Jerusalem as divinely inspired satire. It is the comic picture of the way God's grace punctures our pretensions of power, the heavenly mockery of human might, the divine antidote to arrogant pride. The picture of Jesus parading into Jerusalem on a donkey can become the grace-filled invitation for each of us to get down off of our high horses and walk with Jesus in the way of healthy humility, which can bring healing to the broken place of pride in our lives.

The Latin root for the word *humility* (*humilitas*) is *humus,* which literally means "soil or dust." The word itself provides the visual reminder of the common dust of humanity from which all of us come. The church offers a tangible reminder of this on Ash Wednesday, when the dust of last year's palm branches marks the sign of the cross on our foreheads and we hear the words, "Remember that you are dust, and to dust you will return." At the same time, it conveys the image of the soil out of which healthy, living things grow. If, as Gregory the Great said, unhealthy pride is the cancer that produces sin, humility is the soil in which virtue grows.

A strange thing happened to the people who saw Jesus in that Palm Sunday parade. At first, they may have gotten the joke. Perhaps they even laughed at it. But as they looked into the face of the man on the donkey, some of them remembered the prophecy of Zechariah. At least that's what happened for Matthew, who clearly intends for us to see this event through the lens of the prophet's vision:

> Rejoice greatly, O daughter Zion!
>   Shout aloud, O daughter Jerusalem!
> Lo, your king comes to you;
>   triumphant and victorious is he,
> humble and riding on a donkey,
>   on a colt, the foal of a donkey.
> He will cut off the chariot from Ephraim
>   and the war-horse from Jerusalem;
> and the battle bow shall be cut off,
>   and he shall command peace to the nations;
> his dominion shall be from sea to sea,
>   and from the River to the ends of the earth.
>   (Zechariah 9:9-10)

Perhaps, for one brief shining moment, they caught a glimpse of the radically different kind of ruler. Perhaps they saw the divine King, the humble liberator who would come, not on the back of a charging stallion, but on the back of a borrowed donkey. And perhaps we can see what Matthew saw: the gracious Savior who comes, not on the high horse of human power, but in magnificent weakness; the compassionate Lord who rules not in pretentious pride, but in gracious humility; the "Prince of Peace" who rejects the world's addiction to the myth of redemptive violence, and calls the nations into the way of reconciliation and peace. Here, at the end of Jesus' story, he comes into Jerusalem just the way Phillips Brooks described the way he came to Bethlehem:

> How silently, how silently the wondrous gift is given;
> So God imparts to human hearts the blessings of his heaven.
> No ear may hear his coming,
> But in this world of sin,
> Where meek souls will receive him still,
> The dear Christ enters in.
> ("O Little Town of Bethlehem," *The United Methodist Hymnal*,
> no. 230)

The people who lined the road to Jerusalem that day knew what we, in our sanest moments, know. Something deep within us knows that the only way to enter the human heart is not by way of force or power, but by way of humble, self-giving love. In response, they spread the cloaks on the road as a symbol of the way they were offering themselves in homage to him. They waved palm branches, which, since Judas Maccabaeus in 160 B.C., had been the sign of their hope of liberation. And they shouted the desperate cry of utterly helpless people, "Hosanna! God, save us!"

Jesus' Palm Sunday parody of power declares that this world will be saved from evil and sin not by what the world calls power, but by the divine, self-giving, reconciling love that was revealed at the cross. The broken places in our lives and the brokenness in this world will be healed not through human ingenuity, power, or pride, but through genuine humility; the kind of humility that grows out of "a sane estimate" of our capabilities in the light of the grace God offers to all of us; the kind of humility (*humus*) that becomes the life-giving soil in which a healthy life and healthy relationships can grow.

One of the most poignant moments in the history of the United States Congress occurred on March 1, 1945, when President Franklin Delano Roosevelt came to present his report on the Yalta Conference. The chamber was packed for a joint session, along with the members of the Supreme Court and the President's cabinet. In honored tradition, the doorkeeper announced the arrival of the President. The door opened. A shocked silence swept through the chamber when they saw the President of the United States seated in a wheelchair. FDR's polio had always been the open secret that was carefully hidden from view. One writer called it "a splendid deception." With tremendous exertion, he had always "walked" into the chamber supported on the arm of a colleague. It was the first time anyone had seen him in this condition. For the first time, he did not stand behind the podium but came down to sit behind a small table on the floor.

Then he spoke. "I hope you will pardon me for the unusual posture of sitting down during the presentation of what I want to say, but I know that you will realize that it makes it a lot easier for me in not having to carry about ten pounds of steel around on the bottom of my legs."

At that point, the entire body erupted into sustained applause. Seated on the front row, Frances Perkins, the Secretary of Labor and Presidential confidante, broke into tears. Looking back on that moment, she said, "It was the first reference he had ever made to his incapacity, to his impediment. . . . He was actually saying, 'You see, I'm a crippled man.' He had never said it before and it was one of the things that nobody ever said to him. . . . He had to bring himself to full humility to say it" (*No Ordinary Time*, Touchstone, 1994, page 586).

Presidential historian Doris Kearns Goodwin described the response: "Rather than lessening their regard for him, as Roosevelt had always feared it might, this glimpse of Roosevelt's vulnerability only magnified the power and charm of his personality" (*No Ordinary Time*, page 587). In the President's humility, they found strength.

The crowds along the road may have laughed at the sight of Jesus on the donkey on that Sunday morning, but no one was laughing at the cross on Friday afternoon, the place where, as Helen Kromer wrote, "the knee is bent in humility / In the face of our utter futility" (*For Heaven's Sake*, Williamson Music, 1961, page 7). The humility of Jesus puts to shame all the things we identify as pride, position, and power, revealing each of our lives in the nakedness of our common humanity.

In the end, of course, the joke is on all of us, any of us, each of us, when we take ourselves too seriously and think that we can somehow save ourselves and save our world with anything less than the undeserved, unearned, unmitigated, unexpected mercy, grace, and forgiveness of God revealed at the cross.

In 1980, during some of the darkest days in the struggle against Apartheid in South Africa, Peter Storey preached a Good Friday sermon at Central Methodist Mission in Johannesburg entitled

"These Wounded Hands Are God's." He invited his congregation of wounded, often broken people to see in the wounded, broken hands of Jesus "God, reconciling the world, and you, and me . . . reaching out through all our sin, reaching into all our lostness, reaching across all our failure and forgiving and healing and drawing us to Godself. It is our God who says, 'Come, touch my hands, wounded and torn; and you will be whole'" (*With God in the Crucible,* Abingdon Press, 2002, page 90).

There is, after all, only one way of salvation, only one way toward healing for the broken places, only one way to find grace in the dark places, only one way to enter the kingdom of God. It is the way of that guilty criminal who hung naked and helpless on a cross beside Jesus and said, "Lord, remember me when you come into your kingdom" (Luke 23:42, adapted). The only way to find healing for the deadly power of sinful pride is the way of humility. The cross is the place where all of our high horses die.

There's an old country proverb that says, "If the horse is dead, dismount." The invitation to every last, lost, prideful one of us is to get off our high horse and come, just as we are, to the cross. There, and there alone, we will find strength for every broken place in our lives.

CHAPTER TEN

Endurance: Strength for the Long Haul

Were I to describe the blessing I desire in life, I would be happy in a few but faithful friends. . . . Thus would I pass cheerfully through that portion of my life which cannot last always, & with resignation wait for that which will last forever.

—*Meriwether Lewis,* Undaunted Courage: Meriwether Lewis, Thomas Jefferson, and the Opening of the American West

Like a Shakespearean tragedy, the heroic story of the friendship of Meriwether Lewis and William Clark comes to a heartbreaking end. Lewis had always been prone to what Thomas Jefferson described as melancholy. Today we'd probably diagnose him as being manic-depressive and put him on medication. But in his companionship with Clark, he found the strength and courage to lead the Corps of Discovery across the American frontier to the Pacific Ocean. After the expedition, however, Lewis's life began to spiral downward.

On his way to Washington in the fall of 1809, he was drinking heavily, using drugs, deeply depressed, and "at times deranged in mind." He had attempted suicide twice. One of his companions reported that Lewis would frequently "Conceipt [conceive] that he herd me [Clark] coming on, and Said that he was certain [I would] over take him. That I had herd of his Situation and would Come to his releaf" (*Undaunted Courage,* Touchstone, 1996, page 473, spelling from the original).

But Clark never arrived. On October 11, Lewis stopped for the night at Grinder's Inn, about seventy miles from Nashville, Tennessee. His hostess said that as the sun was setting, he sat on the porch staring "wishfully toward the west." Perhaps he was reliving the time when he and the Corps of Discovery overcame every obstacle, survived every storm, and accomplished a task that seemed impossible. Or perhaps he was looking west, searching the horizon for any sign of the arrival of William Clark. Lewis had told Mrs. Grinder that if Clark knew of his difficulties, he was confident that he would be on the way to help him. The sun set beyond the mountains. During the night, Mrs. Grinder heard two gunshots. She rose to see Lewis staggering from his room. He told the servants, "I am no coward; but I am so strong, [it is] so hard to die." Shortly after sunrise, he was gone (*Undaunted Courage,* pages 473-75).

The final days of the apostle Paul's life offer a hopeful contrast to Lewis's tragic end. Paul was an old man by now. He wrote to his young friend Timothy, "The time of my departure has come." In brilliant contrast to the darkness that closed in around Lewis in his final hours, Paul looked back on his life's journey and declared, "I have fought the good fight, I have finished the race, I have kept the faith." Instead of focusing on the past, he was anticipating the future. As if he were looking toward the rising sun, he saw on the horizon the "crown of righteousness" that was waiting for him at the end of his journey (2 Timothy 4:6-8).

Meriwether Lewis or the apostle Paul—how would you like to come to the end of your journey? When you come to the last days of your life, wouldn't you like to look back over your life with something like Paul's satisfaction with what has been, and something like his hope for what lies ahead?

I told the story of Waller McCleskey's death in my book *Passion, Power and Praise* (Abingdon Press, 2000). He was a faithful Christian gentleman and a longtime member of our church. I'll never forget standing beside his bed less than an hour before he died and hearing him say, "It's been a great life." Given the alternatives, I'd like to come to the end of my journey and say something like that.

Here's my point. The life of faith is not a short sprint; it's a long marathon. The kind of faith with which Paul concluded his life is not something we pick up at the end of the journey. It is the result of specific patterns of spiritual discipline which, if practiced over time, strengthen us for the long haul.

It's not often that a preacher quotes the German philosopher Friedrich Nietzsche, who is remembered for declaring that "God is dead." But he also wrote these words: "The essential thing 'in heaven and earth' is . . . that there should be a long obedience in the same direction; there thereby results, and has always resulted in the long run, something which has made life worth living" (*Beyond Good and Evil*, trans. Helen Zimmern, 1907, Section 188, pages 106-9, as quoted in *A Long Obedience in the Same Direction*, InterVarsity Press, 1980, page 13).

Nietzsche may have been wrong about the death of God, but he was right about what makes life worth living. It's like running in a marathon. It's "a long obedience in the same direction." The grace that strengthens us in our broken places continues to strengthen us for the long haul.

When my walking buddies and I are exercising on Tampa's Bayshore Boulevard, we are often overtaken by a serious runner who slows down to chat with us. The 2007 Chicago Marathon was her sixth marathon and, as it turned out, her hardest yet.

It was unusually hot in Chicago that day. So hot, in fact, that they shut the race down after three hours. One runner died. Several hundred required medical care. Here's the way my runner friend described her experience in a letter to the people who had supported her:

> A marathon (26.2 miles) is not just a physical endurance test; it is also a test of spirit, emotion, heart, and determination. In my past marathons, I have relied most heavily on the spirit and emotion beginning at mile 22 or so. In those last four miles, my body is just coming along with my mind, heart, and spirit. But not in Chicago! At mile 16 my body started feeling very tired and exhausted. My feet were on fire from the sun heating up the asphalt, my head felt heavy and dizzy, and I had a bit of nausea.
>
> What kept me focused and motivated? Thoughts about family and friends who have battled cancer, some losing the battle, their pain and suffering. . . . Thoughts of young kids who don't have a chance to run a 5K race, play ball, and live a normal life. . . . Thoughts of each of you and your generous contributions to Moffitt Cancer Center, and the race to cure cancer and one day, prevent it!
>
> Each of you comes with me in my marathons on a list that I carry in the pocket of my running shorts. In Chicago, I pulled out that list and read your names more times than in the past. You continue to provide me with the inspiration and motivation to endure the challenge. So once again, a huge THANK YOU for getting me across the finish line!

The next time I saw her on the Bayshore, I asked, "Are you glad you did it?" She laughed and shouted back, "Oh, yeah! It was worth it!" And off she ran.

How do we find strength to make it over the long haul? It's a lot like running the marathon. My friend said that she drew on the strength of spirit and the reminder that she was not alone. In the race of discipleship, we are sustained by the Spirit through the disciplines of prayer, scripture, and worship. Like runners in a marathon, we are also strengthened by other Christ-followers who encourage us along the way.

When historian Stephen E. Ambrose attempted to describe how the Corps of Discovery survived their perilous pilgrimage to the west, he pointed to the way the men, and one Native American woman, were in it together. Each member of the Corps was dependent upon every other one. They had determined that "they would triumph, or die, as one" (*Undaunted Courage*, page 246). It's no wonder that when Lewis faced his darkest hours, his mind turned back to the friend who had been with him on that long journey.

My story is that "I get by with a little help from my friends," as the Beatles sang. My friends have been there for me in the most difficult places of my journey, and I have tried to be there for them. We are in this thing together.

On one hand, Paul's final words to his friend Timothy are a reminder that the life of faith is like running a marathon. It's a long obedience in the same direction. But there's a word of urgency in Paul's letter too. It's the kind of urgency with which Lewis looked for Clark to come to his aid.

Paul was a prisoner in Rome. It was autumn. The warmth of the Italian summer was gone, and the damp chill of winter was beginning to penetrate his cell. He made this very practical request in verse 13: "When you come, bring the cloak that I left with Carpus at Troas" (2 Timothy 4:13). Later, Paul adds urgency to the request when he writes, "Do your best to come before winter" (4:21).

In the late 1940s and early 1950s, Clarence McCartney, the pastor at First Presbyterian Church in Pittsburgh, was one of the best-known preachers in America. One fall he preached a sermon on this text from 2 Timothy, entitled "Come Before Winter." This sermon became so popular that the church board requested that he repeat it every fall. And he did it for thirty-seven years!

McCartney described autumn as "the perfect parable of all that fades." He said that "every autumn brings home the sense of the preciousness of life's opportunities—their beauty and their brevity." He pointed to the practical urgency in Paul's request. If Timothy didn't get across the Mediterranean before winter set in, he would have to wait until spring. If Timothy waited, Paul would spend the cold winter without his cloak. There was a good chance that by the time Timothy got there, Paul would be gone. McCartney said, "There are some things which will never be done unless they are done 'before winter.' Before winter or never!" (*Christianity Today*, October 22, 1976, page 18).

His words bring back to my mind these lines from "The Rubaiyat of Omar Khayyam," the English translation of a selection of old Persian poems, which I was required to memorize in junior high school:

> The Moving Finger writes; and, having writ,
> Moves on: nor all thy Piety nor Wit
> Shall lure it back to cancel half a Line,
> Nor all thy Tears wash out a Word of it.

"Come before winter" is the reminder that opportunities come and opportunities go. Pass them up today and they may not come again tomorrow. There are decisions to be made, letters to be sent, loves to be expressed, wills to be written, disciplines to be adopted; and unless they are done today, they may never be done at all.

One of my best friends in Orlando died of cancer at the age of thirty-eight. His wife said that John's death taught her that you have to take the cookies when they are passed. Some things have to be done "before winter" or they may never be done at all.

There's a very practical word there for every follower of Jesus Christ. If we want to reach the finish line and be able to say with Paul, "I've won the race"; if we want to look back on a life that has been "a long obedience in the same direction," we have to start living that way right now. Now is the time to start following Christ. Now is the time to practice those spiritual disciplines which, if practiced over time, will strengthen us for the long haul. Now is the time to connect with Christian friends who will be there for us along the way.

The Reverend McCartney closed his sermon with this challenge to his congregation:

> Once again, then, I repeat these words of the Apostle, "Come before winter"; and as I pronounce them, common sense, experience, conscience, Scripture, the Holy Spirit, and the Lord Jesus Christ all repeat with me, "Come before winter!" Come before the haze of Indian summer has faded from the fields! Come before the snow lies on the uplands and the meadow brook is turned to ice! Come before the heart is cold! Come before desire has failed! Come before life is over and your probation ended, and you stand before God to give an account of the use you have made of the

opportunities which in his grace he has granted to you! Come before winter! (*Christianity Today*, October 22, 1976, page 22)

William Clark didn't get to Meriwether Lewis before he died. We don't know for sure if Timothy got to Rome before winter. My guess is that he packed up his things, picked up Paul's cloak, and headed off to Rome as soon as he received Paul's request. The one thing we know for sure is that this day, and every day, is the time for us to find the grace that will strengthen us for the long haul.

CHAPTER ELEVEN

Suffering: Making Sense of Suffering

*Before crosses used to frighten me—I used to get goose bumps at
the thought of sufferings—but now I embrace suffering even
before it actually comes, and like this Jesus and I live in love.*

—*Mother Teresa,* Mother Teresa: Come Be My Light

Robert Frost gave powerful imagery to a fundamental principle
of life that we all too easily forget. He described the two roads that
"diverged in a yellow wood." Unable to be one person and travel
both roads, he made his choice:

> I took the one less traveled by,
>   And that has made all the difference.
> (*Modern American Poetry*, Harcourt, Brace and World, 1962,
>   page 188)

It makes a difference what road we choose. Some of us most of
the time and most of us some of the time are like the Cheshire cat
that Alice met in her journey through Wonderland. When Alice
asked which road she should take, the cat asked, "Where do you
want to go?" When Alice said she didn't know, the cat replied that
in that case, it really didn't matter what road she chose; if she
didn't know where she was going, any road would get her there.

Luke located the place where the roads diverged for Jesus when he wrote, "When the days drew near for him to be taken up, he set his face to go to Jerusalem" (Luke 9:51). Luke used a very strong Greek verb to describe Jesus' decision to go to Jerusalem. Jesus knew where he was going, and he knew what it would mean. "The Son of Man must undergo great suffering, and be rejected by the elders, chief priests, and scribes, and be killed, and on the third day be raised" (Luke 9:22).

A little farther down the road, Jesus healed a boy whose condition was beyond the ability of the disciples to heal. Luke records that "everyone was amazed at all that he was doing." But then Jesus spoke words that must have sucked the air right out of the room: "Let these words sink into your ears: The Son of Man is going to be betrayed into human hands" (Luke 9:43-44).

Jesus' announcement of his betrayal left everyone who heard it absolutely speechless. Luke says that the disciples "were afraid to ask him about this" (Luke 9:45). My guess is that they weren't just afraid; they were scared stiff! But if most of the disciples were like most of us, and if they had mustered up the courage to ask their questions, my guess is that their questions would have gone something like this: "Jesus, what kind of sense does it make for you to go to Jerusalem if you know what's waiting for you? What sense is there in walking straight into rejection, suffering, and death if you can avoid it?"

The question many of us ask at many of the places where the roads diverge in our lives is the question of suffering. After three decades of pastoral ministry, I can say that the question of suffering, particularly undeserved or innocent suffering, is the soul-level question that breaks the faith of more people than any other question I know. Something deep within us searches for an answer. What's the sense in suffering?

I have a friend who is a highly respected surgeon. Across the years he saw so much suffering, confronted so many seemingly insoluble conditions, that he had nearly given up on his faith. Some years ago I was privileged to be a part of an experience that renewed his commitment to Christ and reenergized his faith. But while I was working on this chapter of the book, we received word that one of his children was struck by an incurable and potentially terminal disease. The pain and injustice of this unwarranted suffering has broken his heart and once again caused him to wrestle with deep questions about his faith.

He is not alone. There are, I suspect, some favored few followers of Christ who never go through the kind of wrestling that my friend does. There may be some who never experience doubt in the face of suffering and pain. But they are the exception. Most of us, who are sensitive to the brokenness in our lives and in the lives of others, often confront the haunting question: What's the sense in suffering?

A young scholar once asked a wise rabbi, "Why do you always answer my questions with a question?" The rabbi replied, "Why do you ask that question?" Just the way a good rabbi answers one question with another question, I want to invite you to explore the question of suffering by asking some critically important questions about this moment when the roads diverged for Jesus.

First, what did Jesus do with suffering?

The shocking answer is that Jesus chose suffering. He chose the way of the cross. The Gospels do not portray Jesus as the helpless sufferer of unfortunate circumstances. He was not the passive victim of inevitable fate. Suffering, rejection, and death were the direct consequences of Jesus' intentional decision to participate in God's redemption of the world by choosing the way of self-giving love. In the wilderness, he was tempted to take other, more comfortable, more socially acceptable ways; the ways of power, position, and self-protection; ways that our culture would call "success." Instead, he "set his face" for Jerusalem and headed directly into the vortex of rejection, human suffering, sin, and death.

Across the first half of the twentieth century, Leslie Weatherhead was one of the primary spiritual leaders in Great Britain because of his unflinching attempt to communicate the core truths of the Christian faith in an increasingly secular culture. In his classic book *A Plain Man Looks at the Cross,* he said that the suffering and death of Jesus reveal that Jesus "willingly committed himself to some mighty task, costly to him beyond our imagining, but effecting for all men a deliverance beyond their own power to achieve" (*A Plain Man Looks at the Cross,* Abingdon Press, 1945, page 71). During Lent each year, I find myself returning to his description of the way Jesus chose the road that led to the cross:

> The stage was set by evil hands; the circumstances were produced by evil men; but the hero was not their victim but their Master, and the passion play carries his meaning, not theirs. The

"must" and "ought" came, not from Herod or Caiaphas or the Pharisees, let alone from Judas, but from God himself, to whose perceived will the heart of Christ said, without faltering, Yea, and Amen. (*A Plain Man Looks at the Cross*, page 58)

This made absolutely no sense to Peter. Luke's Gospel was written after Peter had become one of the leaders of the early church. Some suspect that Luke may have been trying to protect Peter's reputation by omitting his reaction to Jesus' words. But Mark, the earliest Gospel, hangs it out there in front of us: "Peter took [Jesus] aside and began to rebuke him. But turning and looking at his disciples, he rebuked Peter and said, 'Get behind me, Satan! For you are setting your mind not on divine things but on human things' " (Mark 8:32-33). I can understand why Luke might shy away from recording that conversation. It was not a very flattering portrayal of the man who became the rock upon which the church would be built!

Rebuke: that's a shocking word to describe Peter's instant reaction to the direction Jesus had chosen to go. One commentary calls it "a theological response to Jesus' outrageous declaration that shatters all previous conceptions of what the Messiah would do and be" (M. Eugene Boring and Fred B. Craddock, *The People's New Testament Commentary*, Westminster John Knox Press, 2004, page 145). We won't begin to understand the tension between Peter and Jesus at this moment until we feel the gut-level outrage in Peter's rebuke of the one he has just called Messiah. It's the same gut-level reaction that arises in most of us when we are confronted with the road that leads toward suffering. It doesn't make any more sense to us than it did to Peter.

But notice what happened. Mark used exactly the same gut-level word to describe the way Jesus responded to Peter. Jesus turned on Peter, and turned Peter's assumptions inside out, when he "rebuked" him.

There could hardly be a more dramatic description of the totally opposite ways in which Peter and Jesus faced the suffering that awaited Jesus in Jerusalem. Peter set his mind on human things—things like self-protection, self-affirmation, and self-sufficiency. But Jesus set his mind on going to Jerusalem in self-sacrificing obedience to the call of God.

Two roads diverged that day. From a strictly human point of view, the only thing that made sense to Peter was to avoid suffering, to escape rejection, to deny pain. But Jesus told Peter that he was setting his mind in exactly the wrong direction. God's way of dealing with suffering is not to deny it, but to face it; not to avoid it, but to confront it; not to escape it, but to enter into it. God's way of saving the world is not to run from the world's suffering, but to redeem it.

Dr. Allen Verhey teaches at Duke University with a special interest in medical ethics. In his book *Reading the Bible in the Strange World of Medicine,* Verhey says that one of the challenges in the current practice of medicine is that "modern 'compassion' wants to put an end to suffering—and by whatever means necessary." He says that this approach is based on the expectation "that the world should be, right now, the sort of place where suffering can be avoided, where we need not suffer for anything or with anyone." Commenting on Peter's rebuke of Jesus, Verhey writes, "Peter wanted to learn from Jesus how suffering could be removed, not how it could be shared" (*Reading the Bible in the Strange World of Medicine*, Eerdmans, 2003, page 101). Verhey continues:

> Jesus knew better. He taught his disciples not how to avoid suffering but how to share it. The good news is that God shares the suffering, that God does not neglect or ignore the anguished cry of human suffering. The good news is that Jesus made the human cry . . . his own. The good news is that God raised this Jesus up and spoke the last word over the whole suffering creation. (*Reading the Bible in the Strange World of Medicine*, page 121)

The gospel way to make sense of our suffering is to face it, to name it, and to bring it into the presence of the One of whom the prophet Isaiah said, "He was wounded for our transgressions, / crushed for our iniquities; . . . and by his bruises we are healed" (Isaiah 53:5).

Here's the second question: What does Jesus expect us to do with suffering?

The answer is just as shocking to us as it was to the disciples: "Then he said to them all, 'If any want to become my followers, let them deny themselves and take up their cross daily and follow me'" (Luke 9:23). Two roads diverge. There's no bypass around the intersection. The only way to follow Jesus is to follow him in the way of cross-shaped obedience and self-giving love.

Luke adds a word here that doesn't appear in Mark's Gospel. The word is *daily*. Some scholars say that's because Mark was written when the first Christians were facing severe persecution. To take up the cross and follow Jesus could literally mean being nailed to a cross as a martyr. Luke was written some years later, when persecution was less likely. In Luke, Jesus calls us to take up the cross in the ordinary places of our daily lives; to discover what it means to follow Jesus into the ordinary brokenness, fear, hurt, pain, and suffering of our very ordinary, daily lives.

Let's be very clear that following Jesus in the way of cross-shaped suffering does not mean becoming some sort of neurotic masochist who goes around looking for or attracting rejection, pain, and suffering. That's another kind of emotional brokenness that needs to be healed. The suffering that Jesus knew he would face in Jerusalem was the way toward a greater end. It was the inevitable consequence of his obedience to God's call in his life and was the way in which he would fulfill God's saving, healing, life-giving purpose.

I once heard William Sloane Coffin tell his congregation at The Riverside Church in New York that the great tragedy of life is not that we suffer, but suffering that never gets redeemed. Mother Teresa expressed the same conviction when she said that "suffering in itself is nothing; but suffering shared with Christ's Passion is a wonderful gift" (*Mother Teresa: Come Be My Light,* Doubleday, 2007, page 146). The suffering that awaited Jesus was sacrificial suffering that would lead to redemption. Jesus chose to enter the way of suffering because he was confident that it was also the way that led to resurrection. But he was not the first person to walk this road.

In his study of *The Jesus Way,* Eugene Peterson takes us to the most offensive story in the Bible. It's the story of the way God called Abraham to take his son—as the text emphasizes, his "only son"—Isaac, to Mount Moriah and offer him as a sacrifice (see Genesis 22:1-19). Most of us are tempted to either spiritualize the life out of this story or to avoid it completely.

Peterson didn't try to sanitize the story, but he did give me a new way of entering into it. He pointed out that this story is not dropped in out of nowhere. It does not come at the beginning, but rather, at the culmination of the long story of Abraham's journey of faith. From the time God called him to leave behind his home in Ur and follow God to a land he did not know, the life of faith was not something Abraham did with his brain, but something he did with his feet. Faith meant acting in absolute trust and active obedience to the God who had called him, confident that the end result of that trust and obedience would be the blessed life that God had promised. Abraham's life of active obedience was marked by the sacrifices he made along the way.

> Altars built at many a crossroads, a life of repeated sacrifices, each sacrifice an act of discernment, separating the chaff of illusion from the wheat of promise. . . . Habits of relinquishment became deeply ingrained in Abraham. . . . But every leaving was also a lightening of self, a further cleansing of the toxins of acquisition. A life of *getting* was slowly but surely replaced by a life of *receiving* . . . being transformed into a life that abandons self-sovereignty and embraces God-sovereignty. (*The Jesus Way,* Eerdmans, 2007, page 50, italics author's)

That brings Peterson to the foundational biblical principle beneath Abraham's story, and it pointed me in the direction of what it means to "take up our cross daily":

Relinquishment is prerequisite for fulfillment . . . letting go of a cramped self-will opened up to an expansive God-willed life. . . . A sacrificial life is the means, and the only means, by which a life of faith matures. (*The Jesus Way*, page 50)

Sacrifice was the motif by which [Abraham] had lived for years, the letting go, the leaving behind, the traveling light. . . . Each sacrifice left him with less of self and more of God. Each sacrifice abandoned something of self on an altar from which he traveled onward with more vision, more promise, more Presence. (*The Jesus Way*, page 58)

To follow Jesus in the way that leads through suffering to resurrection is to discover what Paul meant when he used the counterintuitive oxymoron "living sacrifice" (Romans 12:1). The life of discipleship calls for a lifelong pattern of sacrifice, an active obedience to God that is willing to face suffering for the sake of redemption; a letting go, releasing what we have to God in order to receive what God has to give.

Here's the final question: What sense does it make to follow Jesus in the way of suffering?

Jesus answered this question when he said, "Those who want to save their life will lose it, and those who lose their life for my sake will save it. What does it profit them if they gain the whole world, but lose or forfeit themselves?" (Luke 9:24-25).

The way of the cross makes sense when we discover that when we try to *save* our life—when we put all of our energy into protecting our own prerogatives, defending our own self-interest, denying our brokenness and pain—we *lose* it. It's only when we lose our lives in something larger than our own self-interest, when we throw our lives into something like the life of Christ, when we open ourselves to our own suffering and the suffering of others, that we find life, real life, life that can never be put to death.

I am keenly aware that this chapter does not provide simple answers to the complex questions of innocent human suffering; questions that haunt our imaginations far more than they tread the pages of scripture. I wrestle with those questions and can, to some degree, make sense of them. (I reflected on the question of suffering in my book *Passion, Power and Praise: A Model for Men's Spirituality from the Life of David,* Abingdon Press, 2000.) But in this exploration of the broken places in our lives, I am led to the conviction that when we set our face to follow Jesus in the way of suffering for the sake of redemption, we are drawn into an experience of Jesus' presence that may not explain suffering, but that gives us strength to redeem it. In following the one "who for the sake of the joy that was set before him endured the cross," it's possible for us to find the strength to "not grow weary or lose heart" (Hebrews 12:2-3).

Mother Teresa discovered the joy that comes through a lifetime of sharing the suffering of Christ. Brian Kolodiejchuk, who surprised the world by sharing the personal letters that revealed "the long loneliness" (to use Dorothy Day's evocative phrase) in Mother Teresa's soul, pointed out that the depth of her commitment to Christ did not make her "gloomy or despondent." Rather, she was "full of fun" and "enjoyed everything that went on." Kolodiejchuk wrote that "her joy was not just a matter of temperament; it was, rather, the fruit of the 'blessedness of submission' that she lived." Mother Teresa said that when she met someone who was sad, her first thought was that this person was "refusing to give something to Jesus." Kolodiejchuk concluded, "It was in giving Jesus whatever He asked that she found her deepest and lasting joy; in giving Him joy she found her joy" (*Mother Teresa: Come Be My Light,* Doubleday, 2007, page 33).

Two roads diverge in the life of every one of us. One is the way of self-protection that ultimately leads to death. The other is the way of self-giving that ultimately leads to life. The choice makes all the difference.

CHAPTER TWELVE

Death: Light in the Darkest Place

It's wonderful to have a world with an Easter morning in its history. . . . Since life's last word for me is to be Easter, I do not mind if life's latest word for me is a cross.

—*E. Stanley Jones,* Selections from E. Stanley Jones

"It was still dark," John says, on that first day of the week when Mary came to the tomb. For both the writer and readers of the Gospel, that description was more than a pre-Timex way of establishing the time of day. Throughout the Gospel of John, "darkness" describes a world that is closed to or alienated from the presence of God. Darkness is mere existence that is not in relationship with God. Darkness is the condition of the broken places in our world and in our lives. By contrast, light describes life, real life, eternal life, life that is alive with the life of God.

John's Gospel opens with that bold declaration: "In him was life, and the life was the light of all people. The light shines in the darkness, and the darkness did not overcome it" (John 1:4-5). It was a great way to begin the Gospel, but at the Last Supper, when Judas left the Passover table to betray Jesus and thereby put in motion the suffering and death of Jesus, John adds this footnote: "It was night" (John 13:30). John also says that the darkness was closing in when Nicodemus, whom John reminds us had first come to Jesus at night, joined Joseph of Arimathea in taking the body of Jesus down from the cross, wrapping it in linen and spices, and laying it in the tomb (see John 19:38-42). John leaves us, at this point, in the darkness, just the way we leave the church on Good Friday night.

It was, in fact, the darkest of all the world's dark nights—"blacker," James Weldon Johnson said, "than a hundred midnights down in the cypress swamp" ("The Creation," http://web.csustan.edu/english/reuben/pal/chap9/jwjohnson.html#creation). It was the night when the darkness overcame the light, the night when life was swallowed up in death. Of all the world's dark places, there is no place on earth as dark as the grave.

"It was still dark," John says, when the women headed off for the tomb on Sunday morning (John 20:1). Even the joyful *alleluias* of Easter Sunday morning worship cannot drown out the fact that this world still has more than enough darkness for all of us. I saw a bumper sticker that said, "If you aren't utterly appalled, you haven't been paying attention." Anyone who hasn't been appalled at the brokenness of our world and aghast at the painful power of violence, poverty, war, and death in our world just hasn't been paying attention. The way the story opens is a powerful reminder that the way to resurrection is the way of the cross. We have nothing to celebrate on Easter morning if we do not face up to the brutal darkness of death.

"It was still dark," John says, when Mary headed to the tomb. And what she found there—better yet, what she *didn't* find there!—simply blew her away. "The stone had been removed," John says (20:1). The grave was empty! The body was gone! There was nothing there but the linen cloths that had wrapped up the broken, bloody, lifeless corpse of Jesus.

I love the women in the Resurrection narratives. The men in the stories can be a little flaky, but the women are something else! Mary was a hardcore realist. She's a lot like all of us who have been conditioned to evaluate everything by the deductive method of the scientific process. She quickly gathered the available information, examined the evidence, and came to the only rational conclusion: "They have taken away my Lord, and I do not know where they have laid him" (John 20:13). Three times, in fact, she says it. First to Peter, then to the angels, and finally to Jesus himself, whom she mistakes for the gardener, which had to be one of the most amazing cases of mistaken identity in history.

We might be tempted to ask what, in heaven's name, Mary thought she was going to do with the lifeless body of Jesus. Exactly where did she think she would take it? What made her think she was strong enough to carry the dead weight of a full-grown man, whose body had been strengthened by walking all across the country? But those questions seem never to have crossed her mind. All Mary knew was that she wanted Jesus back the way she had known him. She would rather hold on to his lifeless corpse than face the darkness of life without him.

There is, of course, a sense in which Mary's conclusion was absolutely correct. The tomb had been raided; the grave had been robbed; the body had been taken. But the grave robber was not the gardener; the grave robber was God! The Resurrection was the unexpected invasion of God's light and life into the utterly predictable darkness of death.

And it was right there, in the darkest place of death, in the darkest moment of her life, that Mary met the Risen Christ. Did you notice the way it happened? There was no thunder, lightning, or earthquake. No orchestra playing or mass choir singing Handel's "Hallelujah." No pyrotechnic appearance of an otherwise unearthly Jesus. The earth's new day of resurrection dawned as silently as the sunrise. There was nothing but the gentle sound of a familiar voice saying, "Mary!" (20:16). She heard Jesus' voice calling her by name. And something about that voice, something about the way she heard it, something about the way it penetrated into the deepest, darkest place in her soul, changed everything.

Mary cried out, *"Rabbouni!"* (verse 16). For all of his non-Hebrew-speaking readers, John explains that the word meant "teacher." But it's more than that. The word *Rabbouni* has the first-person personal pronoun built into it. It actually means *"My* teacher." It's like that moment later in the Gospel when the one we call "Doubting Thomas" recognized the nail-scarred hands of the Risen Christ and cried out, *"My* Lord and my God!" (John 20:28, italics added).

My guess is that Mary was never capable of explaining what happened. It was a moment of encounter that moved beyond explanation into experience. It was a profound, personal encounter in which Mary knew the Risen Christ because she knew that the Risen Christ knew her. Right there, in the darkest place on earth, the light broke through, and Mary knew in a way that she would never stop knowing that the light of Christ shines in the darkness, and the darkness will never be able to overcome it.

Mary's natural instinct was to reach out and touch him, hold him, cradle his body in her arms. But Jesus said, "Do not hold on to me, because I have not yet ascended to the Father. But go to my brothers and say to them, 'I am ascending to my Father and your Father, to my God and your God' " (John 20:17).

The Risen Christ had two commands for Mary that morning: "Do not hold on to me" was one. The other was, "Go." The Resurrection challenge for Mary and for every one of us is to stop trying to hold on to the dead Jesus and to start following the Risen One. Jesus calls us to release the past and to go into the future in the power of the Risen Christ. The Risen Christ invites us to leave behind the broken, lifeless, empty places of our past and to step out into a place of healing, wholeness, and life. We are invited to discover what the psalmist meant when he sang, "You have brought us out to a spacious place" (Psalm 66:12). The Risen Christ calls us out of the past and into the future, out of brokenness into healing, out of death and into life.

I have a preacher friend who likes to say that "Easter means that tomorrow is never just another day." The Resurrection means that we can face up to life, not in the fear or denial of death, but in the confidence of life everlasting. We go into the world, not on the assumptions of the death-denying culture around us, but in the confidence that the God "who raised Christ from the dead will give life to [our] mortal bodies also" (Romans 8:11). Living into the new life of the Resurrection means actively following the Risen Christ through life and into death in the sure and certain hope that "as all die in Adam, so all will be made alive in Christ" (1 Corinthians 15:22). Followers of a Risen Christ face the predictable darkness of death in the unflinching confidence that though "worms destroy this body, yet in my flesh shall I see God" (Job 19:26 KJV). We face the inevitable darkness of death in the unexpected light that shines from an empty tomb. With Charles Wesley we are able to sing

> Soar we now where Christ has led,
> Following our exalted Head,
> Made like him, like him we rise,
> Ours the cross, the grave, the skies.
> ("Christ the Lord Is Risen Today," *The United Methodist Hymnal*,
> no. 302)

I turned sixty while I was working on this book. I can't decide if I think that is younger or older than it sounds, but it forced me to face up to the fact that I've already outlived my father by more than a year. I knew he was young when he died with cancer, but he gets younger every year. But he believed in the Resurrection, and the honesty and faith with which he looked his mortality squarely in the face taught me more about dealing with death than anything I learned in seminary.

During one of our last visits, a longtime business associate came to see him. I remember the way they talked about everything except the thing that mattered most: they talked about everything except his death. As this friend rose to leave, he shook my father's hand and said, "Well, Ves, we can always hope for a miracle." My father accepted his words as a well-meaning attempt at encouragement on the part of a longtime friend who had respected but never understood my father's faith. After the friend left the room, my father turned to me and said, "You know, it's hard for some of my friends to understand that resurrection is a miracle, too. I'm grateful I don't have to have all my miracles on this side of the Resurrection." That's the way he lived, and that's the way he died, in the hope that Paul described in the letter to Corinth:

> Listen, I will tell you a mystery! We will not all die, but we will all be changed, in a moment, in the twinkling of an eye, at the last trumpet. For the trumpet will sound, and the dead will be raised imperishable, and we will be changed. For this perishable body must put on imperishability, and this mortal body must put on immortality. When this perishable body puts on imperishability, and this mortal body puts on immortality, then the saying that is written will be fulfilled: "Death has been swallowed up in victory." / "Where, O death, is your victory? / Where, O death, is your sting?". . . Thanks be to God, who gives us the victory through our Lord Jesus Christ. (1 Corinthians 15:51-57)

Then Paul added this postscript: "Therefore, my beloved, be steadfast, immovable, always excelling in the work of the Lord, because you know that in the Lord your labor is not in vain" (verse 58).

It was still dark when Mary came to the tomb that morning. And there is still more than enough darkness in this world for all of us. But in the darkest place on earth, Mary found the light that shines in the darkness, and the darkness will never be able to overcome it. In the darkness, she met the Risen Christ; and we can meet him there too.

CHAPTER THIRTEEN

Sorrow: A Broken Hallelujah

Somewhere between suffering and hope lies poetry, somewhere between the Cross and the Resurrection lies the "cold and broken Hallelujah."

—Mary Veling, "The Failed Messiah: A Broken Hallelujah," quoting Leonard Cohen, "Hallelujah"

I began this book by saying that I would invite the reader into some of the broken places in my own life. Fulfilling that promise, this chapter invites you into one of the most painful losses I have ever faced. I share the story as one broken person sharing with another broken person both the pain of his loss and the strength he is finding to face it.

The telephone call came totally by surprise. Nothing could have prepared me for it. The voice on the other end of the line was familiar. I had known Jack since he was a kid in elementary school. I had followed his journey through high school, where he became a world-class swimmer, then to college, where he trained for the Olympics. I walked with him through his struggle to discern God's call for his life, encouraged him in seminary, performed his marriage service, stood with him when he was ordained, and now shared the joy of being his colleague in ministry.

Jack's father, Glenn, and his mother, Ginger, were some of the first people my wife and I met when we moved to West Orange County, Florida, to launch a new congregation in the orange groves nestled between Walt Disney World and Universal Studios. Beyond building the church, we built a friendship that had only grown deeper and stronger in the years since we left that community. Their home became our home for our daughter's wedding, and they celebrated with us when our first grandchild was born. We vacationed together, cheered for the University of Florida Gators football team together, ate more meals, shared more laughter, and cried more tears together than we could ever begin to count.

It was Jack's voice on the phone, but it was a voice broken with tears. "A terrible thing happened," he said. There was a long, agonizing pause as he gasped for breath and sobbed until he was able to say, "Dad had a heart attack today, and he died." I don't know if it was because he was having such a difficult time saying it or because I was having such difficulty hearing it, but I had to ask him to repeat the words before they could begin to sink in. He told me what had happened and said, "He loved you so much!" And I loved him, too.

At the age of seventy-one, Glenn was one of the healthiest guys I knew. He ate well, exercised rigorously, and kept his regular checkups with his physician. He still worked part-time in the land development business, but he and Ginger loved to travel. The place he loved the most was their cabin in the North Carolina mountains, where he would escape the Florida summer heat.

And that's where it happened. Walking along a country road in the mountains, Glenn collapsed and was gone. Jack was calling from New York, on his way back from England, where he was working on a Ph.D. on John Wesley's theology. The family was headed toward Orlando to meet there. Stunned, almost unable to speak, I drove home and blurted the words out of my mouth that knocked the wind out of my wife's lungs: "Glenn died today."

We were waiting outside the door of their home when the family arrived, ready to fall into each other's arms and allow our unashamed tears to speak what words could never say. And then, of course, the invitation came. They asked me to preach in the memorial service if I wanted to do it.

Immediately I had two equally clear and conflicting thoughts. *On one hand,* I wondered, *how could I pass up the opportunity to preach a sermon that Glenn wouldn't be able to critique?* We all laughed about the way he always seemed to have plenty of advice for all the people he loved, particularly the preacher! Earlier in his life, he had considered going into the ministry and still held high expectations for anyone who stepped into a pulpit. *On the other hand,* I thought, *how can I preach when I feel so broken?*

The question was still hanging in the air when the family's current pastor came to plan the service. In the process of the conversation, we all laughed at our own "Glenn stories," because he was a joy-bringer of the first order. At one point the pastor turned to me and said, "Well, Jim, if you want to speak, I know you would have lots of great stories to tell."

Those words haunted me during the night. I'm not very good at something that felt like a combination of a roast and an after-dinner toast. When I awoke the next morning, I was sure of one thing: If I was going to do anything in the service, I would have to preach. Glenn would not have it any other way. He was a thoughtful, faithful layperson who believed in the importance of preaching and was never satisfied with pabulum in the pulpit. He was never satisfied with simplistic answers to complex questions of life and faith. His critique of my sermons was always a way of encouraging me to go deeper. I knew that Glenn would want me to preach.

When I walked into the house the next morning, Jack met me at the door. His first words were, "Jim, if you want to participate in the service, we want you to preach." And so, I knew what I had been called to do. As I attempted to prepare what would clearly be for me one of the most difficult sermons of my life, I was drawn to the Forty-second Psalm:

> As a deer longs for flowing streams,
>   so my soul longs for you, O God.
> My soul thirsts for God,
>   for the living God. . . .
> My tears have been my food
>   day and night,
> while people say to me continually,
>   "Where is your God?"
>
> These things I remember,
>   as I pour out my soul:
> how I went with the throng,
>   and led them in procession to the house of God,
> with glad shouts and songs of thanksgiving,
>   a multitude keeping festival.
> Why are you cast down, O my soul,
>   and why are you disquieted within me?
> Hope in God; for I shall again praise him,
>   my help and my God. . . .

Deep calls to deep
   at the thunder of your cataracts;
all your waves and your billows
   have gone over me.
By day the LORD commands his steadfast love,
   and at night his song is with me,
   a prayer to the God of my life. . . .

Why are you cast down, O my soul,
   and why are you disquieted within me?
Hope in God; for I shall again praise him,
   my help and my God.

So, here's the sermon I preached. I include it in this book as a grateful witness to a faithful friend—I am sure you have people like him in your own life—and as an expression of the way God's grace met me in one of the most painful broken places of my life.

"A Broken Hallelujah"

We know how the psalmist felt when he said, "The waves and billows have gone over me. . . . Tears have been my food night and day."

I need to say right up front that Glenn's emotions were just as close to the surface as mine, but he didn't have to stand up here and let everyone see them. Glenn was not ashamed of his tears, and we don't need to be ashamed of ours. The truth is that, like the psalmist, we gather here in worship as broken people.

But in his brokenness, the psalmist remembers going to worship with the throng, singing with glad songs of thanksgiving. Through his tears, he finds just enough faith to sing a broken hallelujah.

"A broken hallelujah." When Jack called with the word of Glenn's death, I remembered those words which had been spoken by a staff member in a meeting that morning. I had never heard that phrase before. When I Googled those words—something Ginger would have had to do for Glenn!—I found a song by blues singer Leonard Cohen, and a theological essay in which the writer said, "Somewhere between suffering and hope lies poetry, somewhere between the Cross and the Resurrection lies the 'cold and broken Hallelujah'" (Mary Veling, http://dlibrary.acu.edu.au/research/theology/ejournal/aejt_4/veling.htm).

I'm grateful, in times like these, that there is room in our faith for brokenness. I'm grateful that biblical writers saved a place in scripture for "the songs of lament," sung by the psalmists and prophets who never hesitated—the way we so often do—to name their grief, anger, hurt, and pain over the utter injustice of their experience. Because of their presence in scripture, I've come to believe that the voice within us that shouts, "This isn't right! It isn't fair! This isn't the way things were supposed to be!" is nothing other than the Spirit of God speaking out of the deepest places of our souls.

In times like these, I'm grateful that Saint Paul said that the Spirit prays within us in groans that are too deep for words. And I'm grateful that we follow a Jesus who wept beside the grave of his best friend. I'm grateful for a God who is with us in our brokenness and tears. And I am grateful that there is room in our faith for a cold and broken hallelujah.

We're here in worship today to sing a broken hallelujah for such a life.

The writer of the epistle of James said that every good and perfect gift comes from God. Glenn wasn't perfect, though Ginger never stopped trying! If she had just had a little more time! His life may not have been perfect, but it was very good. If his life had not been so good, the loss would not hurt so badly.

Hallelujah for the love of a good husband. Hallelujah for the model of a good father. Hallelujah for good leadership in so many good things. Hallelujah, broken as it is, for such a life.

We're here to sing a broken hallelujah for such a friend.

The church has never recognized friendship as a sacrament, but it probably should. After all, it was around that Last Supper table that Jesus said, "I no longer call you servants; I call you friends."

Most of us are here today because we were given the good gift of Glenn's friendship. We know that our lives are more joyful, more productive, and more faithful because of that unearned, undeserved gift. And we know that the pain of our brokenness is a small price to pay for such a priceless gift.

I haven't checked this out with Glenn's favorite Wesley scholar, his son, Jack, but my sense is that while John Wesley knew how to be a great leader, Charles Wesley knew how to be a great friend. If I were organizing a movement, I'd call on John; but if I wanted to hang out in the pub, I'd go for Charles. He wrote a beautiful hymn about Christian friendship:

> If death my friend and me divide,
> Thou dost not, Lord, my sorrow chide,
> Or frown my tears to see;
> Restrained from passionate excess,
> Thou bidst me mourn in calm distress
> For them that rest in thee.
>
> I feel a strong immortal hope,
> Which bears my mournful spirit up

Beneath its mountain load;
Redeemed from death, and grief, and pain,
I soon shall find my friend again
Within the arms of God.

Pass a few fleeting moments more
And death the blessing shall restore
Which death has snatched away;
For me thou wilt the summons send,
And give me back my parted friend
In that eternal day.
("If Death My Friend and Me Divide," The United Methodist
Hymnal, no. 656)

We're broken people, singing a broken hallelujah for such a friend. And finally, we sing a broken hallelujah for such a faith.

There's no way to explain who Glenn was without affirming what he believed. Glenn's life was built on the rock-solid foundation of a constantly growing, constantly maturing relationship with Jesus Christ; a relationship that was rooted in scripture, nurtured in prayer, celebrated in worship, and expressed through the gifts he shared with all of us.

We are here, somewhere between suffering and hope, somewhere between the cross and Resurrection, somewhere between the dark valley of death and the bright hope of eternal life, to affirm the faith in which Glenn lived, the faith in which he died, and the faith in which we claim for him the hope and promise of the Resurrection. We are here, in the presence of God, to claim for ourselves the faith of the psalmist who said, "Hope in God; for I shall again praise him, my help and my God."

It's no secret that Glenn and Ginger had different tastes in music. The Winter Park (Florida) Bach Festival was not exactly Glenn's idea of a good time. His tastes ran more in the direction of the Nitty Gritty Dirt Band, singing the old gospel song that asks,

> Will the circle be unbroken
> By and by, Lord, by and by?

And by faith, we dare to believe that the answer is, Yes! One day, by God's grace, the circle will be unbroken. One day our broken hearts will be healed. And one day we will sing an unbroken hallelujah in the presence of the Risen Lord. Amen.

That's what I preached. That's what I believe. And that's where I am finding the strength to face this very broken place in my life.

CHAPTER FOURTEEN

Hope: Turning Sorrow into Joy

Joy and woe are woven fine,
A clothing for the soul divine;
Under every grief and pine,
Runs a joy with silken twine.

—William Blake, *"Auguries of Innocence"*

G. K. Chesterton, the rotund and not particularly child-friendly British journalist, novelist, and theologian, once observed the way small children find unbridled joy in repeating the same thing over and over again. Here's what he said:

> A child kicks his legs rhythmically through excess, not absence of life. Because children have abounding vitality, because they are in spirit fierce and free, therefore they want things repeated and unchanged. They always say, "Do it again," and the grown-up person does it again until he is nearly dead. (*Orthodoxy*, Doubleday, 1952, page 60)

Every grandparent knows that Chesterton's thesis is empirically true. Shortly after our granddaughter, Julia, learned to walk, she discovered that she could climb up onto the hearth in our family room, a whopping eight inches above the floor. Her ever-watchful grandmother told Julia to hold on to her finger so she could jump down without falling flat on her face. And, of course, Julia wanted to do it again, and in no time, she wanted her grandmother to jump with her. Julia called out, "Gamma, jump!" And Gamma obediently climbed up onto the hearth, grasped Julia's hand, and jumped down to the floor. Then it was "Gampa, jump!" And so Gampa crawled off the sofa, climbed up onto the hearth, and started jumping with her, down to the floor. Then (as if you didn't know where this story would go!) it was "Gamma, Gampa, jump!" So Gamma and Gampa *both* got up onto the hearth, each held one of Julia's hands, and they all started jumping off the hearth.

After doing this about 150 times, Gamma and Gampa were starting to get a little weary of the game; but for Julia, every leap was like a new adventure, filled with all the exuberance of the first one.

Based on such an observation, Chesterton wrote one of his best-known paragraphs about the nature of God:

> Perhaps God is strong enough to exult in monotony. It is possible that God says every morning, "Do it again" to the sun; and every evening, "Do it again" to the moon. It may not be automatic necessity that makes all daisies alike; it may be that God makes every daisy separately, but has never got tired of making them. It may be that [God] has the eternal appetite of infancy; for we have sinned and grown old, and our Father is younger than we. (*Orthodoxy*, page 60)

Chesterton identified pessimism as "an emotional half-holiday" and called joy "the uproarious labour by which all things live" (*Orthodoxy*, page 60).

The writer of Psalm 126 celebrated the God who has "the eternal appetite of infancy"; the God who is always ready to "do it again";

the God who never gets weary of healing broken places, turning tears into laughter and sorrow into joy. The psalmist looked back on the long years of Israel's brokenness during the exile in Babylon. He remembered the way refugees returning to Jerusalem thought it was all a dream; almost too good to be true.

> When the LORD restored the fortunes of Zion,
>   we were like those who dream.
> Then our mouth was filled with laughter,
>   and our tongue with shouts of joy. (Psalm 126:1-2)

On the basis of what God had done in the past, the psalmist prayed for God to do it again in the present.

> Restore our fortunes, O LORD,
>   like the watercourses in the Negeb.
> May those who sow in tears
>   reap with shouts of joy.
> Those who go out weeping,
>   bearing the seed for sowing,
> shall come home with shouts of joy. (Psalm 126:4-6)

The writer of the Thirtieth Psalm claimed the hope that "weeping may linger for the night, / but joy comes with the morning" (Psalm 30:5). In a time when tears had been his food night and day (see Psalm 42:3), the psalmist remembered going up to the Temple "with glad shouts and songs of thanksgiving" (Psalm 42:4). On the basis of that memory, he declared, "Hope in God; for I shall again praise him" (42:5). G. K. Chesterton could have been speaking of the Israelites' faithful hope when he said, "They are in spirit fierce and free, therefore they . . . say, 'Do it again.' "

Ernest Hemingway got it right when he said that sooner or later, the world breaks all of us. The night of weeping comes to everyone. There are times when we feel defeated because our best efforts can't seem to put Humpty Dumpty together again. Battered by daily headlines that overwhelm us with the brokenness of this world and persistently reminded of the broken places in our own lives, there are long nights when we wonder if the dawn will ever come; lonely hours of loss when we doubt that we will ever sing a song of joy again. When we walk through the dark, lonely valley of the shadow of death, we know what Chesterton described as "the downward drag of all things into an easy solemnity." It's what Emily Dickinson was feeling when she said that "after great pain, a formal feeling comes" (*Modern American Poetry,* page 100).

And what then? When hearts are broken, dreams are shattered, and hopes are dashed to the ground, how can we find the God who meets us in that broken place to perform the alchemy of grace that turns tears into laughter and sorrow into joy?

The psalmists described a joy that is nothing less than a miraculous work of God. Listen to what other people were saying about the returning exiles:

> Then it was said among the nations,
>   "The LORD has done great things for them."
> The LORD has done great things for us,
>   and we rejoiced. (Psalm 126:2-3)

The return from exile was not something this band of dejected refugees could ever have done for themselves. It was an unimaginable, unanticipated, unadulterated work of God. It's like the old country proverb that says if you see a turtle sitting on a fence post, you know it didn't get there by itself. Joy is an undeserved, unearned, and largely unanticipated work of divine grace in the lives of God's people.

The English poet William Wordsworth wrote, "I have felt / A presence that disturbs me with . . . joy" (from "Lines Composed a Few Miles above Tintern Abbey"). I felt that disturbing joy in the aftermath of the story I told and the sermon I shared in the previous chapter.

I can find no joy in the ruthless way death robbed us of Glenn's life and friendship. I am all too keenly aware of the joyless vacuum that ought to be filled with his laughter. Any glib, religious affirmation about how joyful Glenn must be in heaven falls on my soul with a cold, icy thud. Because I believe in the Communion of Saints, I believe that Glenn somehow continues to be present with and aware of the people he so deeply loved. In that case, I cannot believe that even in the new life of the resurrection, he does not share the ongoing pain of those he left behind. Maybe those are the scars that even the resurrection can't remove.

And yet, there is soul-rending joy in the memory of just how good Glenn's friendship was. There is unexpected joy in the continuing witness of the way God used him in the lives of his family and friends. As a preacher, I am disturbed with joy in knowing that the sermon I offered was the best gift I could give as an act of praise. And there is joy in the hope that one day the night of weeping will be over and the dawn of joy will come. One day the circle will be unbroken, and we will have plenty of time to tell our stories and celebrate God's presence together. It's an odd, disturbing joy that can only be the gift of God's grace.

The psalmist believed in joy that emerges out of pain.

Considering the situation, some of the most surprising words Jesus ever spoke had to be at the Passover table on the night before he died, when he told the disciples, "You will have pain, but your pain will turn into joy. . . . In this world you will face persecution. But take courage; I have conquered the world!" (John 16:20, 33, adapted). He compared the kind of joy he promised to the pain of a woman in labor.

When we were preparing for the birth of our first child, we went to the kind of natural childbirth class that was typical in the early 1970s. In the first session, the idealistic birthing coach told us that we would never use the word *pain*. When Carrie Lynn was on the way, my wife was in labor for eighteen hours. I can tell you, it was pain! But just the way Jesus promised, it was pain that was soon overcome by the joy of a child entering the world.

Jesus never denied the very real pain involved in the life of discipleship. In fact, he said that participating in the kingdom of God is an inherently painful business. It goes with the territory. I've discovered that the closer I get to Jesus, the more deeply I feel the very real pain, suffering, injustice, and brokenness of the world. Following Jesus takes me deeper than I really want to go into the broken places in my own life and the pain-soaked lives of others.

Bishop William Willimon was surprised when he found a member of one of his most affluent congregations washing dishes in a homeless kitchen. The bishop asked, "Have you always enjoyed working with homeless people?" The man barked back, "Who told you I enjoyed working with homeless people? Have you met any of these people?" Somewhat surprised by the reply, the bishop asked, "Then how did you get here, washing dishes at seven in the morning for a bunch of homeless people?" The man replied, "I got put here by Jesus, that's how. How did *you* get where you are?" (William H. Willimon, *Who Will Be Saved?* Abingdon Press, 2008, page 126).

Far from offering us an escape from pain, Jesus often leads us deeper into it. He never promised to do away with pain, but he promised that our pain would be overcome by joy—joy of which "happiness" is a vacuous shadow.

When, after four years of impatient waiting and persistent persuasion, Mother Teresa was finally given permission to establish the Missionaries of Charity Sisters, she made it perfectly clear that their purpose was not to escape pain but to share it. Her biographer wrote, "Mother Teresa did not want to avoid sacrifice or eliminate it from her life or the lives of her followers. . . . She knew their suffering would bear fruit" (*Mother Teresa: Come Be My Light*, page 140). The joy with which she offered compassion and love to the poorest of the poor demonstrated the truth of some of the last words of Pope John Paul II: "All human suffering, all pain, all infirmity contains within itself a promise of salvation, a promise of joy" (quoted in *The Christian Century*, May 17, 2005, page 53).

The joy the psalmist experienced and the joy that Jesus promised is not some sort of frothy happiness that floats across the surface of human suffering. It is, in fact, joy that comes out of the same place as pain. The gospel is clear that the only way to joy is the way that goes through sorrow. The only pathway to laughter is the one that is sometimes blinded by tears. The only way to resurrection is the way that leads to a cross. The only way to find new life is to face up to the reality of death. As far as I can tell, the divine alchemy that changes sorrow into joy is always a work of the Spirit of God. It is always new life that comes out of pain.

The sad news of our battered lives and our broken world is that we are all broken. We have all sinned and grown old. The good news is that our Father is younger than we are. The God who has an infinite appetite of childhood is always ready to do it again, to turn tears into laughter, sorrow into joy, and death into new life.

Barbara Brown Taylor is one of the most highly respected preachers and teachers in the Episcopal Church today. She confessed that early in her ministry, one of her least favorite pastoral tasks was taking Communion to the local nursing home on the poor side of town. Most of the residents spent the day strapped into their wheelchairs staring unresponsively at the television. Half of them slept through the entire twenty-minute service she would lead. When she tried to serve the bread and cup, some looked at her as if she were a burglar. On a particular day, one woman sang, "Row, row, row your boat" out loud while Taylor was reciting the liturgy. Taylor said that with her arms raised over the bread and wine, she felt as if she might as well be flying a kite.

In an attempt to get their attention, she clapped her hands and shouted, "What shall I read from the Bible today? What would you like to hear?" The commotion settled down just long enough for one frail voice to be heard through the noise: "Tell us a resurrection story." Suddenly, the fitful congregation became silent. Like a grandchild pleading with her grandparents to "Do it again," another patient and then another repeated the request, "Yes, tell us a resurrection story" (*The Preaching Life,* page 65).

God's grace is always available to strengthen us in the broken places. And so our broken hearts cry out, "Do it again! Do it again!"

Questions for Personal Reflection or Group Discussion

Introduction

1. Ernest Hemingway said, "The world breaks everyone and afterward many are strong at the broken places." How do those words speak to you?

2. What difference does it make for you to discover that "the biblical message is carried by story and celebrated with song"? How have you seen God at work in your own story?

3. What do you hope to experience in this study? Because this book is personal, you are invited to be personally engaged in it. You may wish to use a journal to record your reflections and to keep track of the ways your story intersects with the stories that are shared here.

1. Scar Lover: The Signs of What We've Been Through

1. How do you respond to the name "Scar Lover"? Do you have scars on your body that remind you of what you have been through?

2. How would you have felt if you had been present in the upper room on that first Easter evening? What questions would have been on your mind?

3. Does it seem odd to you that the Risen Christ still bore the scars of crucifixion? Why? What difference do those scars make in your understanding of the Resurrection?

4. In what ways can you identify with Thomas?

5. How have you experienced God's grace in acknowledging the scars in your life? Where have you found strength to face them?

2. Sin: How Things Get Broken

1. How do you respond to the comparison of Humpty Dumpty with the story of Adam and Eve in the book of Genesis? What is your understanding of "The Fall"?

2. What is your personal definition of the word *sin*? How have you experienced it?

3. How do you respond to Augustine's guilt about taking the pears from a neighbor's orchard? Is there any way you can identify with his feelings?

4. How do the four assumptions about sin (sin breaks relationships, sin distorts goodness, sin is deadly, sin can be redeemed) speak to your experience?

5. What does "salvation" mean to you? How have you experienced it?

3. Temptation: Where the Wild Things Are

1. Where have you met "the wild beasts of temptation"?

2. Read aloud the wilderness story from Matthew 4:1-11. What words or images from this story speak most directly to your experience?

3. Have you been baptized? If so, how does your baptism remind you of who you are as a follower of Christ? If not, what are

your thoughts and feelings about making that commitment in your faith?

4. When have you experienced the words of scripture as a source of strength in a time of temptation?

5. How has God's grace met you "in territory held largely by the devil," as Flannery O'Connor put it? How have you been strengthened to face temptation?

6. Read the words of Martin Luther's hymn "A Mighty Fortress Is Our God." What would it mean for you to claim that strength in your temptations?

4. Lust: Taming the Fatal Attraction

1. What is your definition of *lust*? How have you experienced it?

2. How can you distinguish, as Augustine put it, "the calm light of love from the fog of lust"?

3. Read the story of David and Bathsheba in 2 Samuel 11–12. What is most disturbing to you about this story?

4. Where can you find yourself in the story of the adulterous woman and the judgmental crowd in John 8:2-12?

5. What do you think about the practical steps that are suggested in this chapter (get honest, get forgiven, get help, get smart, get healed)? Is there a way these suggestions could be helpful for you?

6. How have you seen God's grace at work in the broken place of lust?

5. Greed and Envy: When Enough Isn't Enough

1. What is your response to the question that opens this chapter: What would you be willing to do for $10 million?

2. Read Luke 12:13-34. Do you really believe that "one's life does not consist in the abundance of possessions" (verse 15)? How does that statement fit in with the values of the culture around us?

3. What's the difference between being "evil" and being "foolish"? Why do you think Jesus said the rich man was foolish?

4. Walk through the three invitations Jesus offers in this chapter. What difference do you think they would make for you?

5. John Wesley called his followers to do the following: "Gain all you can. Save all you can. Give all you can." How have you applied those practices to your life?

6. Sloth: To Care and Not to Care

1. How does the word *sloth* make you feel? What does that word mean to you? How do you respond to the author's definitions of the term?

2. Read the story of the good Samaritan in Luke 10:30-37. What surprises you in this story? With which character can you identify most closely? How do Jesus' words make you feel?

3. Read the story of Jesus visiting Mary and Martha in Luke 10:38-42. What surprises you in this story? With which character can you identify most closely? How do Jesus' words make you feel?

4. Which of the two just-mentioned stories do you need to hear most directly right now? Have you learned how to keep the message of both stories in balance in your life? Explain.

5. What does it mean for you "to care and not to care"? What do those words say to you about balance?

7. Gluttony: Super-sized Sin

1. What signs of gluttony have you seen or experienced? What is your definition of *gluttony*?
2. Read 1 Corinthians 6:19-20. What does it mean to you to hear Paul say, "Your bodies are members of Christ" (1 Corinthians 6:15)?
3. What are the practical implications of Paul's teaching about discipline and freedom found in 1 Corinthians 6:12?
4. How do you understand the affirmation, "The deepest hunger in our lives is always the hunger and thirst for God"? How have you experienced that hunger?
5. What choices do you need to make to find healing for the broken place of gluttony in your life?

8. Anger: The Froggy Gremlin in All of Us

1. Is your anger the blazing kind or the brooding kind? Explain your answer.
2. When have you experienced appropriate anger? When have you felt the kind of anger Jesus felt? How did you express it?
3. When has anger become sinful for you? What motivated your anger?
4. How is anger connected to forgiveness? How can the words of Desmond Tutu regarding forgiveness help you to deal with your anger?
5. Where have you experienced God's grace in dealing with anger?

9. Pride: Let Your High Horse Die

1. Have you ever thought of the Palm Sunday procession as "downright laughable; a Monty Python sort of satire; an absurd

parody of what the world calls real power"? What difference does it make for you to see it that way?

2. How would you describe the difference between sinful pride and healthy self-respect? When have you taken yourself too seriously?

3. Where have you observed God's grace as "the divine antidote to arrogant pride" that "punctures our pretensions of power"?

4. Reread Zechariah 9:9-10. How does the prophecy of Zechariah help you understand Jesus' entry into Jerusalem?

5. How do you respond to the story of Franklin Delano Roosevelt's message to Congress? How would you have felt if you had been there?

6. What will it mean for you to get off your high horse of pride?

10. Endurance: Strength for the Long Haul

1. What captures your attention in the contrasting stories of Meriwether Lewis and the apostle Paul?

2. How would you like to come to the end of your life? Describe the conditions.

3. Read again Nietzsche's words about "a long obedience in the same direction." How do these words speak to you?

4. Where do you find strength for the marathon of faithful living? Who are the people who encourage and support you? Have you ever let them know how important they are to you?

5. In light of the urgency of Paul's request for Timothy to "Come before winter," what do you need to do today? What opportunities are before you now that may never come again?

11. Suffering: Making Sense of Suffering

1. How do you deal with the question of undeserved or innocent suffering?
2. Reread Leslie Weatherhead's words about the way Jesus went to the cross. What difference does it make for you to know that Jesus chose the way of suffering? How can you identify with Peter's rebuke of Jesus?
3. What difference does it make to know that Jesus shares in our suffering?
4. What would it mean for you "to take up the cross in the ordinary places of our daily lives"?
5. What is your reaction to the story of Abraham's sacrifice of Isaac (see Genesis 22:1-19)? Drawing from the words of Eugene Peterson, what would you need to sacrifice in order to exchange "a cramped self-will" for "an expansive God-willed life"?
6. How have you experienced God's grace in times of suffering in your life?

12. Death: Light in the Darkest Place

1. How does the Gospel writer John's use of "light" and "darkness" speak to you? When have you experienced them?
2. Read the Resurrection story from John 20:1-18. How can you identify with Mary in this story?
3. How have you experienced the light that shines in the darkness? When have you felt the presence of the Risen Christ in some dark place in your life?
4. How does the hope of resurrection strengthen you to follow Christ today?

5. Read 1 Corinthians 15, which deals with resurrection. How does the message in this scripture change your understanding of life and death?

13. Sorrow: A Broken Hallelujah

1. What is the greatest loss you have experienced? Retell that story, as the author has told his story of loss.
2. Read Psalm 42. How can you identify with the psalmist?
3. How does the phrase "broken hallelujah" speak to you?
4. How do you respond to the idea that "the voice within us that shouts, 'This isn't right! It isn't fair! This isn't the way things were supposed to be!' is nothing other than the Spirit of God speaking out of the deepest places of our souls"?
5. Reread the words of Charles Wesley's hymn "If Death My Friend and Me Divide." When have you shared a friendship like that?
6. How does the promise that the circle will be unbroken strengthen you in the face of sorrow?

14. Hope: Turning Sorrow into Joy

1. When have you experienced the kind of childlike joy G. K. Chesterton describes?
2. Read Psalm 126. Have there been times when the psalmist's words here could have been your words?
3. When was the last time you felt a presence that, to paraphrase William Wordsworth, "disturbed with joy"? Where have you experienced the presence of the God who can turn tears into laughter and sorrow into joy?

4. How have you experienced the joy that comes out of the same place in the human soul as pain?
5. What would it take for you to be open, ready, and responsive for God to "do it again" in your life? Where is Jesus leading you?
6. What difference has this study made in your life? How have you experienced strength in your broken places? How can you share that strength with others?